Making Jewelry from Polymer Clay

To my soulmate, Olivier, and my children, Sara, Antoine, and Quentin, for having accompanied me during the creation of this beautiful project.
Website: http://cristalline.blogspot.com

Thanks to: http://www.perlesandco.com/
Thanks to: Cléopatre, fabriceclabaut@colles-cleopatre.com

I must thank my editors, Colette Hanicotte and Corinne de Montalembert, in particular, for believing in the integrity of my project.
Thanks to the diligent readers of my blog for helping me realize this project and see it through.
Thanks to Eva M. for her support and availability.

Published by
STACKPOLE BOOKS
5067 Ritter Road
Mechanicsburg, PA 17055
www.stackpolebooks.com

Printed in the United States of America

10 9 8 7 6 5 4

First edition

Photographs by Amelie Vuillon (www.plusnature.com)
Cover design by Wendy A. Reynolds

Cataloging-in-Publication data is on file with the Library of Congress

ISBN 978-0-8117-0694-0

SAFETY NOTES
- Do not eat or drink while working with polymer clay, and wash your hands thoroughly after using it.
- Use your polymer clay tools only for working with polymer clay, nothing else. Remember that clay will harden after it has completely cooled.
- There are many different brands of polymer clay—some should not be used by children—and the temperature for baking them will vary from one brand to another. Follow the manufacturer's instructions carefully; these instructions are on the packaging.
- Never exceed the temperature and duration indicated for heating the clay—doing so can create noxious fumes. It's best to use an oven thermometer as well as a timer.
- Never use a microwave oven to heat polymer clay.
- Children should be supervised by an adult.
- Consult a doctor in the case of ingestion of polymer clay, wounds contaminated with the clay, or the inhalation of toxic fumes caused by overheating.

Making Jewelry from Polymer Clay

Sophie Arzalier

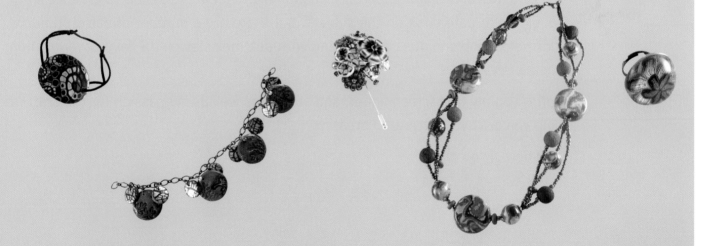

STACKPOLE
BOOKS

Foreword

Invented in the 1930s, polymer clay has never stopped evolving and today offers infinite jewelry project possibilities.

Sold in the form of pliable, colored bars, this plastic material is available in different compositions. Though there are differences between the various brands (Fimo, Kato Clay, Sculpey, and Premo are a few of the best-known brands), the principle is the same: Polymer clay hardens after it is heated (or "baked") in a standard oven. The colored bars can be combined, so the color palette is infinite, as are the effects you can create by mixing. Polymer clay retains textures and patterns—even the most delicate—and is compatible with a number of paints and finishing products. And unused clay lasts for a long time if it is stored properly.

Fun and easy to use, polymer clay is accessible to even young crafters and allows for the creation of numerous unique projects. The continuing development of polymer clay products and accessories and the expanding amount of information about using the clay, available online especially, might make it seem impossible to produce a thorough, up-to-date book on the subject. But there are a number of basic, standard, indispensible techniques for working with polymer clay, and I have covered them completely here.

I offer you my tricks, techniques, and advice—as well as my passion for the craft—to help you discover the joys of creating.

And now . . . go play!

Contents

Introduction

Working with **Textures**

Working with **Different Materials**

Working with **Canes**

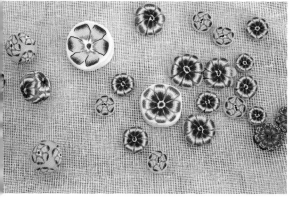

Using a Mix of **Techniques**

Introduction

Materials

Polymer clay

Different brands of blocks of different sizes are available. Although there are some variations among them, all harden when heated in a standard oven. Certain brands can be mixed together.

In theory, the three primary colors (blue, red, and yellow) along with black and white are sufficient to create any color imaginable. Doing this requires a bit of familiarity with color theory (explained on page 132). Today, though, you can find a rainbow of premade colors as well as clay dyes, which greatly simplify color creating.

Preserving the clay

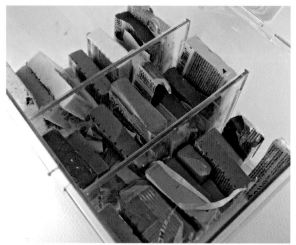

Polymer clay can be preserved quite nicely at room temperature, but if you don't want your individual clay blocks or canes to dry out too quickly or stick together, it's best to keep them separate. The best way to do this is to wrap unused pieces of clay with cellophane (the kind used by florists is ideal). Don't use aluminum foil for this; it sticks to clay and can be difficult to remove.

ADVICE

To firm up clay that is too soft, let it rest several hours on a piece of paper, which will absorb excess grease.

Place your canes—which are the rods of clay that contain the designs you create—vertically in a deep clear box. Cover the bottom of the box with a sheet of cellophane.

Keep excess bits of clay in another airtight box. It's helpful to group them by color. These bits can be used in the future as a base color for marbling. Clay scraps can also be used to create the cores of beads that you want to be a certain diameter. You can cover this core with a thin pattern or a colored layer.

Baking

Always follow the baking instructions on the clay's packaging. Never exceed the temperature indicated and always ventilate the room after baking. A standard kitchen oven can be used safely—just don't cook food the same time as you are heating clay. Never use a microwave oven to bake clay.

Tools

The tools you use for clay modeling and baking should be used only for these purposes. They must not also be used to prepare or handle food. Clean your workspace often, and wash your tools and hands with soapy water as you work, especially between handling richly pigmented colors. Wash everything again when you're finished.

• Roller

A small metal tube or PVC pipe is perfect for clay. Avoid wood, which has a tendency to get dirty very quickly. You can also find special rollers for polymer clay in craft stores.

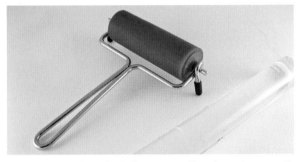

Red rubber rollers nicely fuse cane slices to make smooth pieces with a velvety finish. Transparent acrylic rollers allow you to see your work as you do it and clean up easily with a swipe of a cloth or in soapy water.

• Cutting blades

For the beginner, one cutting blade (an X-Acto knife or old-style razor blade) will suffice, but you will probably soon want to invest in more suitable blades made especially for cutting clay. These are longer lasting and will allow you to create very thin slices. Get blades most suitable for the type of cutting you do the most:

- *Tissue blades* are large, long, firm blades for cutting blocks and straight lines.
- *Flexible blades* are thin, supple blades for cutting clay thinly and cutting curved lines.
- *Ripple blades* are corrugated for creating interesting wavy effects.

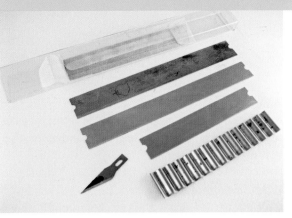

The blade allows you to handle pieces of clay without deforming them. To lift clay from the work surface, pass a blade between the clay and the table, leaving the clay piece on the flat surface of the blade.

Remember that sharp blades can be dangerous and must be used carefully. Younger crafters using blades should always be supervised and assisted by an adult. Put away your blades after use.

• Work surface

Working with clay on a piece of smooth transparent glass is ideal. Glass can be cleaned with a swipe of a cloth, and you can slide a pattern or measuring chart underneath it. If the glass is small, it can also go directly into the oven, which keeps you from having to handle your creation before baking and possibly deforming it.

• Die cutters

You can probably find a number of die cutters in the children's section of a craft store. These work great for many polymer clay projects. If you want to obtain more intricate cutters, metal ones in a variety of shapes and sizes are

often available. Search the bakery aisle, where there might be cookie cutters and accessories suitable for clay. Look for whatever might work—plastic cups, medicine containers, caps (from bottles, pens, shampoo, and so on)—and set them aside for clay projects.

• "Appropriated" tools

Toothpicks, plastic cards (such as ATM cards), needles, cookie and candy cutters, and whimsical punches for scrapbooking can all be used with clay.

• Clay machine

A hand roller works great for beginners, but it usually becomes necessary to invest in a clay machine for more complex projects. The one shown here is very useful for making fine gradations, pieces with perfectly regular thicknesses, and ultrathin sheets.

• Molds

There are many different types–different patterns and different brands. You can also create molds by using small clay sheets to take an imprint of interesting objects (cloth mate-

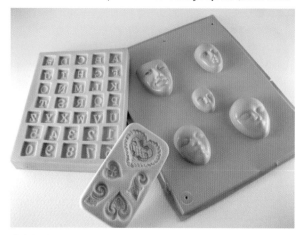

rial, textures, stamps, old buttons, and so on) that you can then harden. Leftover clay will work for this, especially if you lightly sprinkle talcum powder on the object before taking an imprint. You can also buy mold-making silicone material that will allow you to create very precise molds.

• Stamps

In red rubber, silicone, wood, or iron, stamps can be found at all prices, with all sorts of patterns. Look for printing-

press characters or stamps for fabric in wood or brass used for Indian prints.

• Textured sheets

Polymer clay textured sheets are usually made with red rubber or cast plastic. They are soft and very thin and pass

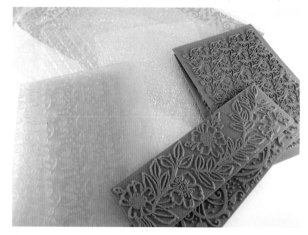

through a clay machine to create a regular and precise texture. You can also use other interesting materials, such as lace, to impart texture to clay, or you can make textured sheets yourself.

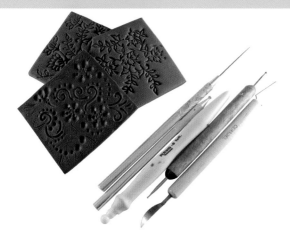

- Top right: powder applied to the stamp and different powder applied with the finger around the pattern
- Bottom left: powder applied to the stamp and the surrounding clay
- Bottom right: powder applied to the stamp and the surrounding clay, which is then sanded to remove some of the color

• Metallic powders

Eye shadow does the job well: It creates metallic or colored sheens, accentuates raised patterns, catches the light, and

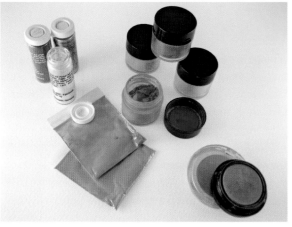

lets the color of the clay come through. When laid down more thickly, it can color an entire piece.

You can also buy specialty powders that are applied directly to raw clay or used as varnishes after hardening.

Powder can create different effects:

- Below, top left: an imprint without powder and powder applied with a finger around the pattern

• Gold or metallic foil

Traditionally used for gilt, foil mixes prettily with polymer clay to create sophisticated effects. Gold foil catches the

light and adds depth; it's a key component of the crackle effect for the project on page 39 and the mokume gane effect for the project on page 65.

• Paints and inks

Oil paints and alcohol inks add wonderful color to translucent clay or liquid polymer. Standard acrylic paint can be applied as a transparent wash or more thickly.

- Top center: powder applied to the stamp and unpowdered clay around it

• Plexiglas plates

Used for attaching silicone stamps in scrapbooking, these plates are very useful for flattening a clay object, scaling down ("reducing") a square or triangular cane, and making round disks.

• Oven

To bake your clay, use an oven–preferably electric, which creates a more even temperature than does a gas oven. Use an oven thermometer during the first bakings to verify that the temperature is correct: If it's too low, the beads will be fragile. If it's too high, tints will darken, and noxious fumes could be created.

Never use a microwave oven–even if you find information to the contrary online. Temperatures are hard to control, and you risk burning the clay and creating other hazards.

Another baking tool is a heat gun. Often meant for use with embossing powders in scrapbooking, a heat gun allows you to quickly heat a coat of liquid polymer or make small repairs in the clay without putting the piece back in the oven. Follow the instructions that come with the gun. You must carefully control the distance from the object and the heating time. And the gun must be set on a stand when it's not being held but is still warm.

Baking aids
• Aluminum foil

Although it's not useful if it comes in contact with clay during heating, you can form foil into a compact ball that

can hold toothpicks to support beads in an oven or as the core of large beads to keep them light.

• Silicone

A range of silicone products that can be heated have useful anti-adherent properties for work with resin and polymer clay. Please note that very thin pieces of silicone can warp in an oven and affect the clay they support.

• Glass or ceramic

Ovensafe glass and ceramic surfaces can support clay during heating, helping you keep fragile pieces from deforming. Perfectly smooth surfaces create a flat plane for bigger pieces–although occasionally air bubbles can get trapped between the clay and the surface and affect the jewelry.

• Lightbulbs

Lightbulbs in varying sizes can be used to support clay as it is baked. The curved surface of the bulb allows you to create curved clay pieces.

Basic techniques

Preparing the clay

To prepare polymer clay for working, warm it up in the palm of your hands and knead it several times until it becomes soft. If necessary, use the clay machine, but be careful to avoid creating air bubbles that could make the piece fragile. To avoid these, cut the clay to a thickness of around $1/8$ inch and pass it several times through the clay machine (or use a hand roller) until the consistency is soft throughout. If your clay crumbles, warm it up in your hands before continuing.

Marbling

This effect is always interesting and adds a sophisticated look to the pieces.

1 Choose two, three, or four clay colors. Remember that the

farther apart from each the colors are on the color wheel, the less they will mix.

2 Roll out long strands of each color then twist them together.

3 Fold the whole thing in half and twist it again. If you continue to fold and twist like this, the finer and more complex your marbling will be.

You can cut your final roll in slices to make tube-shaped or round beads or roll them by hand or with a clay machine

to create marble striping that can be used as is or as part of a patterned piece. Don't forget to save the leftover scraps; they often make very pretty marbled pieces.

Shading

• Without a clay machine

Create two triangular clay sheets as shown below then place them side by side so they form a rectangle. Cut horizontal strips from the rectangle that contain both colors. Knead the strips with your hands, gradually pushing one color into the other to create the shading.

• With a clay machine (the "Skinner Blend")

1 Create a rectangle with two triangular pieces of clay as described above. Note that the more inclined the diagonal that separates the triangles is when the rectangle is hori-

zontal, the more gradual the shading will be. The more this line approaches vertical, the more abrupt the shading will be. Also remember that dark tints will quickly overwhelm lighter tints. Experimenting will help you create varying effects.

2 Fold the rectangle in half horizontally (long end to long end).

3 Run the clay through the clay machine, adjusted to the clay's thickness, with the folded end going in first, parallel to the roller.

4 Run the clay through the machine repeatedly in the same manner. After around twenty passes, the shading should be perfectly even.

• How to make a thin shaded strip

The process is the same as described above, but each time you pass the piece through the machine, adjust the thick-

ness setting so the opening gets smaller and smaller. The thinner the clay is pressed, the more it will elongate, and a strip will be created. Just be careful that it doesn't get too thin or it will tear apart.

• Shaded square canes

Fold the thin strip like an accordion, keeping it at least $3/4$ inch wide (make sure to press out any air bubbles; the bubbles could make little holes in your cane).

• Shaded circular and targetlike canes

To create a shaded circular or targetlike cane, simply roll a shaded strip up. The color you start with will be the heart of the cane. To do the same thing without the clay machine, proceed as follows:

1 Make a light, single-color roll and wrap it in a piece of darker clay, trimming the edges so they meet but don't overlap.

2 Continue to wrap with successively darker strips.

Beads of an even size
• Round or oval beads

Work the clay then create a flat sheet using the clay machine. Use a "cookie cutter" to cut as many square pieces as desired—the larger the cutter, the fatter the beads. Roll the cut pieces in your hands to make them round or oval.

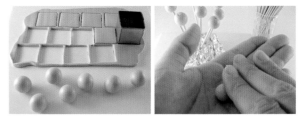

• Round beads with a clay gun

Form round clay pieces of equal size, slightly smaller than the desired final size. Make "spaghetti" with the clay gun (see page 24) then wrap the round pieces with the clay string.

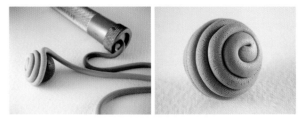

• Cubes

For cubes, start with a round bead and press it between the thumb and the index finger of each hand, turning it on itself as you press. If you want to create sharper angles, use two pieces of Plexiglas or regular glass to press the bead. After hardening, sand the sides smooth.

• Disks

Use the same technique as for round beads then flatten them between two pieces of glass. Or make a sheet of clay of the desired thickness and cut the disks with a cookie cutter. Note that it is much easier to pierce this type of bead after it hardens to limit deformations. It's also best to use a support that can go into the oven.

• Tubes

Make a thin, even sheet with the clay machine. Wrap the sheet around a wooden skewer several times until you get the thickness you want. Twist the skewer carefully so you can pull it out (this is very difficult to do after baking). Bake the piece, then, while it is still warm, cut it into the desired lengths with a rigid blade.

• Tubes with a clay gun

Make "spaghetti" with the clay gun in the desired color and wrap the string around a skewer.

Salt beads

These beads are easy to make and have a unique and interesting look. They can be used alone or mixed with others to create contrast.

1 Roll beads of the desired size and color in table salt. If you use the palm of your hand to do this, the texture will be a bit more pronounced than if you roll the beads in a

bowl. Note that the coarser the salt, the more prominent the markings, which look great on larger beads.

2 Pierce the beads, bake them, and wash them as soon as you remove them from the oven to dissolve the salt.

Round, patterned beads

• Integrated pattern

1 Make a ball with leftover clay (remember that if you cover this with translucent colors, the base color will be visible).

2 Cover the ball with thin slices of cane by placing them side by side. Use a point to push down any part of the inner

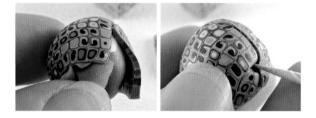

ball that's visible between the slices then gently push the edges of the slices together as needed.

3 Gently roll the bead between your hands to smooth it.

• Spaced pattern

1 Make a cube in the desired color.

2 Cut six thin slices of a patterned cane and apply them to each side of the cube.

3 Press the edges of the slices into the bead until they

are worked into the clay, then roll it lightly in one direction and then another to form a ball without damaging the pattern.

You could also use variations of these techniques, as shown below.

Finishing touches
• **Piercing beads without deforming them**

Before baking
This is meticulous work: The more the clay has been worked, the more easily it can be deformed.

1 Place your beads in a freezer for several minutes before

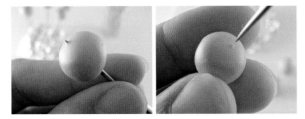

piercing. To avoid fingerprints, wear a thin glove on the hand that will hold the bead. The size of the piercing tool determines the size of the hole, which depends on the thread you will ultimately be using.

2 Proceed in two stages: First, make a hole to the center of the bead by turning the bead on the tool. Make the hole as centered as you can.

3 Then turn the bead and pierce the other side the same way to connect the two holes. If necessary, roll the bead lightly in your hands to restore its shape.

Pierce square beads using the same technique.

After baking
This method is preferable for fragile beads, especially those with raised patterns or metallic powdering. To pierce after

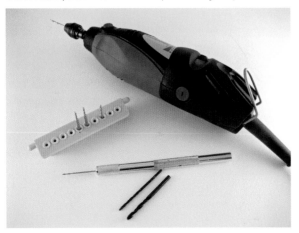

baking, use a mini-drill, which usually comes with bits of different sizes.

ADVICE

On very thin pieces, hold a drill bit and pierce by hand. Just-baked clay is usually flexible enough to do this. Or you can attach the bit to the drill but not turn it on and use it by hand. Use a powered drill on other fragile beads. Keep a good grip on the bead so it doesn't fly away during drilling. Remember that a hole that doesn't go through the center of a bead will cause it to hang unbalanced.

• **Sanding**

If you smooth your work well before firing and are careful to avoid air bubbles, the sanding you'll need to do on a finished piece will be minimal.

1 It's best to use sandpaper meant to be wet. For the backs of pieces and on irregular surfaces, start with 400-grit paper (the lesser the grit, the coarser the paper). Use a light, even, circular motion. Crumple the paper first so it is soft.

2 Follow with 600-grit paper, then 1000-grit, then 1500-grit. This is the minimum level needed for the best appearance. I usually continue to 2000-grit paper for beads that are to be lustrous or matte. (If you plan to varnish your beads, you can stop at 600-grit paper.)

3 Wash sanded beads with soapy water. If your work has raised patterns, scrub it with a soft toothbrush reserved for this purpose.

• **Polishing**

Lightly polishing a well-sanded bead creates a satiny surface; in fact, you can create a shine similar to that created by several coats of varnish.

ADVICE

Surfaces with crackled gold leaf or metallic powders should never be sanded. Beads with fine patterns must be sanded very carefully so they retain their texture. And remember that perfectly sanded beads have a smooth and soft finish that can eliminate the "handmade" look.

There are many methods for polishing polymer beads, and you can find descriptions of them online. Personally, I use a sheepskin disc that I attach to my mini-drill with the aid of a tip that has a screw thread. Wear protective glasses when polishing and hold your bead tightly so it doesn't fly off and get damaged or injure you.

After polishing, wipe the bead with a cotton cloth to remove deposits.

• Varnishing

These tips will help you create a smooth, even coat of varnish:

1 Use some kind of support to hold the beads, and turn them after each coat so the varnish doesn't collect on one side.

2 Use several thin coats rather than one thick coat; a thick coat can alter the underlying color and create an uneven surface. If the first coat retracts and becomes irregular, don't despair: Successive coats will correct the appearance.

3 Varnish beads only when they are completely dry and hardened.

The varnish will hide imperfections and create the most handsome effect on a surface that has been sanded with up to 600-grit paper.

• Resin

I use a two-part crystal resin. Mix the parts thoroughly, without creating air bubbles, then apply the resin with a thick stick to a hardened polymer piece. The clay surface must be perfectly smooth—don't hesitate to sand it with up to 600-grit paper to be certain the resin will adhere completely.

If it is too warm, resin gets too thick to apply. Let it cool a bit. As well, if it is too liquid, let it stand for an hour or so before using. To support the piece to be resined, I use a glass plate coated with a release aid applied with a brush, which prevents the bead from sticking to the plate. For cabochons and rings, the silicone molds with a shiny coating for cooking are perfect. You must be careful to handle pieces to be resined with dry hands—damp spots of sweat will prevent the resin from adhering properly.

• Liquid polymer

A liquid polymer called Kato Polyclay offers results similar to those obtained by using resin. This product is applied with a brush to hardened clay, which is then baked again. Fimo liquid polymer works best with colored glazes and for joining two pieces.

• Glue

Several types of glues will work with polymer:

- *jewelry glue*, for attaching fibers or feathers
- *epoxy glue*, to attach metal preparations to baked clay
- *heat-resistant glue*, which allows you to attach crystal beads, for example, to unfired clay, or attach pieces that have already been formed and baked
- *superglue*, for assembling pieces, polymer against polymer, and for repairs—but remember that superglue must never be used on warm pieces or pieces to be baked as this can create toxic fumes.

Textures

To texturize a surface means to create a raised pattern on the clay with the aid of a stamp, texture tool, or almost anything that imparts an interesting look. Quick and easy, this technique can be used with all kinds of clay forms—canes, salt beads, and so on—and can be varnished or left unfinished.

Ready-made textured sheets are available to use with clay. Thin and flexible, most can pass between the rollers of the clay machine and can be used on both sides of a clay sheet, which creates a positive/negative effect. You'll get the best results if you cool pieces of textured clay in the freezer for several minutes before working with them.

• Textures and acrylic patinas

A raised pattern can be accentuated with metallic powders added with the tip of the finger or with the application of a patina of acrylic paint before or after firing. A wide variety of products are available for creating a range of beautiful effects.

A liquid paint will creep into the valleys of a texture; a thick paint applied with a cloth will color only the raised portions. With these two techniques, you can create a variety of looks.

The base clay is black in each of these examples.
1 White paint wiped off.
2 Silver paint rubbed onto the raised pattern.
3 Brilliant blue-green wiped off then rubbed with gilt paint.
4 Red paint wiped on then rubbed with gilt paint.
5 Terra cotta paint wiped off.

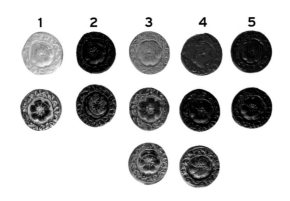

Once the paint is completely dry, you'll want to apply at least one coat of varnish to protect it.

• Creating your own textures

A number of texturing items are available today, but you can also make them yourself at little cost. These have the great advantage of being entirely unique.

There are many easy ways to make your own textured sheets:
- work on "scrap" clay
- use two-part molding silicone
- use a linoleum block
- use a large eraser

The benefit of using scrap is that it is soft and can be formed without carving by using stamps or any other object with an interesting raised pattern (whatever you like!). Molding silicone is soft and easy to texture, too, but its rapid drying time doesn't allow for much refining.

• Disk textured on both sides

1 Prepare two molds of identical size with a pattern that will be different on the two faces of the disk. Make a mark on the side of each mold so you can align them properly.
2 Lightly powder (or dampen) the molds before each use. If you use powder, brush the interior well so the powder isn't clumped.
3 Prepare a piece of clay that's a ⅛ inch thick and place it on the face of one of the patterns.

4 A small dab of liquid polymer on the clay will help it adhere to the mold better. Place the other mold on the back of the clay, making certain your marks are aligned. Press.
5 Give the raised patterns a patina with acrylic paint or leave them raw, according to your preference.

• Creating molds

1 To make a quality mold, take a good thickness of clay and smooth it with a roller. Powder the surface.
2 Press the pattern into the clay with a glass plate so you can create even pressure. Remove the pattern very carefully, then bake the clay. Don't forget to powder it before each use.

❋ ADVICE

Remove one half of the mold and cut away the excess clay while the piece is still adhered to the other half. This will help you keep from deforming the raised pattern. Then very gently pull the clay piece from the mold.

• Making decorative casts

When the pattern of the mold is deep enough and precise, you can make decorative casts that can be applied to the surfaces of a base piece.

1 Push a piece of clay into a powered mold

2 Place a glass plate on the back of the clay and press it until the clay adheres.

3 Turn the plate over and carefully remove the mold then use a thin, sharp blade to slice the textured surface from the excess clay. The resulting cast can then be applied to jewelry.

    A number of casts can be applied to a piece, which you might then enhance with a metallic patina.

Different effects
• Opaque mokume gane

Mokume gane is directly inspired by the ancient Japanese technique of the same name, which consists of combining layers of metals to create colored curves. Instead of metal, we'll use clay.

1 Lay three clay sheets of three different colors on top of each other with the darkest tint on the top. Pass the whole thing through the clay machine set at a thickness of $1/8$ inch.

2 Put this clay on top of another sheet of the lightest color, then texture the clay, pressing a pattern into the clay's dark side.

3 Using a tissue blade—a curved, flexible blade with two handles—carefully "shave" off the raised parts of the texture to reveal the layers of clay underneath.

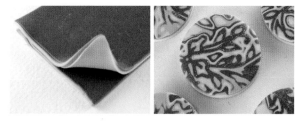

Variation 1

Cut the sheet of three colors in half, and place them on top of each other to create more layers. This can create a kind of halo effect around the elements of the pattern.

Variation 2

Make a shaded sheet of clay and put it on the sheet that has the darker shade on top. This will create a soft pattern with little contrast.

✳ ADVICE

To avoid moving the clay while you are shaving it, work on a glass surface or ceramic tile of adequate size. Be careful not to cut off too much material so that patterns remain visible, dark on a base of light. Remember, too, that sanding during the finishing process will remove more of the surface color.

• Mokume gane with metallic foil

The effects are very different if you blend gilded or silvery foil with translucent polymer clay. To do so, you'll use the technique known as mille-feuille—sandwiching colored clay between thin sheets of translucent clay and, between these, a metallic sheet.

1 Cut the ends of the clay stack cleanly and make small, twisted rolls with the leftovers. With the handle of a tool, make several holes in the stack then insert the rolls.
2 Press the block onto a smooth, rounded surface, such as the side of a glass bottle.
3 Slice off segments of the clay with a thin blade.

✳ ADVICE

To protect the metal within mokume gane jewelry, it's best to varnish the finished pieces. Unvarnished metal can oxidize if it comes into contact with your skin.

• Mokume gane with powders and metallic foil

This method gives mokume gane pieces color and translucency. It works best to use metallic powders for this instead of alcoholic inks because they have a tendency to color the entire piece. (Remember to wear a face mask when working with metallic powders.)

1 First, condition the translucent clay. Make a sheet for each color and apply the powder on them one by one with a brush—this way you can control the amount of powder you use (too much powder and it won't mix well into the clay). Knead the clay well in order to obtain a consistent color.

2 Cover each colored sheet with a gilded metallic sheet then stack them all like a sandwich.

3 Slice off the edges as you did previously, poke holes, then fill the holes with twists of the excess material.

• Hidden Magic

This technique was introduced to the United States by Jenny Patterson.

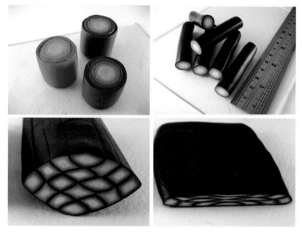

1 Using three different colors (either contrasting or complementary), create three target-style or shaded circular canes, with the lightest color in the center.

2 Wrap these canes with a thin layer of black clay then roll them until they elongate then cut the resulting cord into $1^1/_2$-inch lengths.

Create a clay block by placing the lengths side by side so the ends create a contrasting pattern, as shown. Press the block so it flattens to around $^1/_8$ inch (more informa-

tion on this technique is offered on page 24).

3 Texture the surface of the flattened piece using stamps or dyes. Wooden or brass dies create the best effect because their deep, precise designs stay crisp after cutting.

4 Shave the surface to reveal the layering, keeping the leftover clay (you can use it to make beads).

• Mica shift

Pearly and metallic clays have a base of powdered mica, which creates the illusion of depth on a completely smooth surface.

1 Apply mica to a clay sheet then fold it in half, sealing the powder inside. Run the clay through a clay machine at

least ten times, each time with the fold passing through first, parallel to the rollers. This helps align the mica particles within the clay.

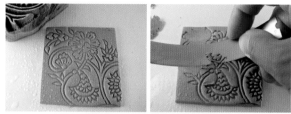

2 Texture the surface of the clay as you wish.

3 Shave off the raised portions of the pattern to reveal the underlying colors. Smooth the surface very gently with a roller.

4 Sand and polish the piece when it's complete. Note that certain pearly white tints become more pronounced after the piece is heated.

• Imitation materials

Surface treatments can give polymer clay the look of a variety of materials. The close resemblance can sometimes be surprising.

Canes

Many polymer clay techniques were inspired by ancient crafts, such as millefiori (which means "thousand flowers" in Italian), used by glassmakers. This procedure allows you to create a long cylinder of clay that contains the same pattern from end to end. When the cylinder is cut into slices, the precise pattern is revealed. The slices are applied to a base, creating elaborate designs. The simplest pattern to create within a cane is a targetlike effect.

The physical properties of polymer clay allow you to adapt this technique to create an almost infinite variety of patterns: geometric or figurative, simple or complex, large or small. It is just a matter of technique, mastery, and practice.

• Reducing a round cane

• Reducing a squared or triangular cane

1 Press the clay toward the center of the cane evenly to elongate the section. Start at the center of the cylinder and work out toward one end, and then the other. Use both hands, pushing the clay down on a smooth work surface; you can also gently stretch the clay with your hands, smoothing from the center toward the ends. As you work, keep turning the cane a quarter of a turn.

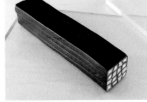

1 Take the round cane in two hands and squeeze the center with your fingers.
2 Turn the cane a quarter of a turn before each squeeze to help keep the shape symmetrical. You want to create an even hourglass shape.
3 Squeeze one of the ends, turning the clay as you do to keep the shape symmetrical. Then squeeze the other end. Your hourglass should now look like an even cylinder.
4 Roll the cylinder gently and evenly on a smooth surface so it gradually gets thinner and elongates.
5 Once the clay is reduced to the size you want, press lightly on any lumps to make the strand as smooth as you can.

Remember to always let a just-reduced cane rest before you cut it. It will be very soft immediately after it's reduced and difficult to slice evenly. If you cannot wait at least one night, put the cane in the freezer to cool it more quickly. Note that some brands of clay blend more quickly, and the precise separation of colors in these might diminish.

2 You might want to use small sheets of Plexiglas to help you reduce a squared or triangular cane. This will help you keep the shape even. These sheets can usually be found in the stamping or scrapbooking sections of a craft store.

• Making canes with a clay gun

The tool known to polymer clay crafters as a clay gun offers ways to create clay canes in an almost infinite number of styles. By varying the quantity of clay used, the order of the colors, the gun tip, and the way the clay is positioned in the gun's tube, you can create many different effects. This technique is very easy to use; the only drawback is that it's almost impossible to create identical canes with a gun.

• Simple canes of concentric circles

Place clay disks of various colors one by one in the tube of the clay gun, as shown. Concentric circles will be revealed when you slice the cane the gun makes. Remember that

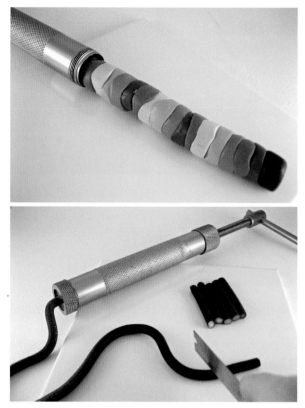

the first disk in the tube will be the color of the outer-most layer.

• Simple spiral cane

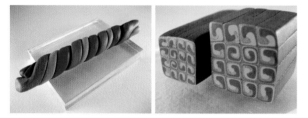

Place strands of clay next to each other then twist them together before inserting them into the tube. Slicing will reveal a spiral design. Note that the final inch or so that comes out of the tube often contains a slightly tighter pattern.

• Complex spiral cane

1 To create a complex pattern of concentric circles, first use the clay gun to make a strand of concentric circles.
2 Cut the strand into 1¹/₂-inch sections then lay the sections side by side on a thin, 1¹/₂-inch-wide sheet of clay.
3 Roll up the sheet carefully so you don't squeeze the sections.
4 Reduce the resulting cane as desired, and let it rest before slicing.

• Complex flower cane

1 Create a complex spiral cane or cane of concentric circles and wrap it with a thin sheet of clay in a contrasting color.
2 Reduce the wrapped cane and cut it into six sections of the same length. Squeeze these sections into teardrop shapes and place them around a targetlike cane with a small diameter.
3 Use translucent clay to make rolls that will fit into the spaces between the "petals."
4 Wrap the entire piece with another sheet of translucent clay and reduce.

• Square grid cane

1 Use the clay gun with a square tip to create square clay strips.

2 Make one large block by laying the strips together as shown. The colors should roughly match the example. Press on each side of the block with Plexglas sheets so the strips adhere to each other. The resulting cane can be used as is or serve as a base for numerous projects, like the flowers and leaves featured in the projects in this book.

• Flower cane

1 Prepare a square grid cane, as described above.

2 Stretch the cane so it elongates but retains its shape.

To do so, turn it on the diagonal and press it, flattening the top and bottom as evenly as possible.

3 Use a roller or a clay machine set at about ⅛ inch to elongate the cane further. You want to create a long ribbon.

4 Cut the ribbon into 2-inch segments, setting aside one segment for the heart of the flowers. Stack the other segments so the colors are all oriented the same way.

5 Round the stack by pinching the sides. You'll need to add a thin roll of clay the same color as the sides to fill in the gap created by the pinching.

• Flower cane with six petals

1 Wrap a flower cane with a thin sheet of dark clay. Reduce the wrapped cane then slice off six equal segments, leaving an inch or so extra.

2 Use the extra cane to make the center of the flower; roll this piece into a spiral.

3 Arrange the six canes like petals, insert the center roll, and trim it.

4 Add rolls of translucent clay between the petals then wrap the entire cane in a translucent sheet. Reduce the cane as desired.

To make a fuller flower, reduce the base cane a little and make the petals thinner.

• Leaf

1 Start by cutting nine slices about 1 inch thick from a flower cane then pinch the two ends of each slice. Arrange them

into a rough leaf shape as shown. Make a stem from a strip of lighter colored clay between two darker colors.

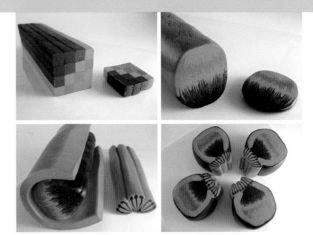

2 Insert the stem and wrap the whole piece with a thin layer of dark clay. Reduce the cane.

3 If, as you reduce, the tip of the leaf grouping becomes rounded, pinch it after reducing to sharpen it.

To make a small bundle of leaves, cut four slices and pinch the ends to shape them. Fill the spaces between

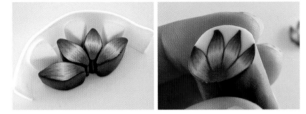

the leaves with rolls of translucent clay, as you did for the flower, but wrap only the top part with a sheet of transparent clay. Two or more of these small bundles placed side by side will create lush foliage.

• Poppy cane

1 From ⅛-inch sheets cut two red squares and one black square, each about 1 inch by 1 inch. Stack them with the

black in the center. Add to the side of the stack a small black cylinder about 1 inch long and the height of the stack. Wrap the entire piece in a ⅛-inch-thick red sheet.

2 Reduce and elongate the stack. Cut it into three equal parts and set them side by side. Add little red clay rolls in the spaces at the top and reduce the whole thing again then cut three canes each about 3 inches long.

3 Pinch the length of each cane, at the base of each stamen, as shown. Set the three parts side by side.

4 To create the heart of the petals, make a red-and-black base flower cane and wrap it in a red sheet of clay about ¼ inch thick.

5 Wrap most of the cane with a thin sheet of black clay— leave the black side of the cane unwrapped, however. Cut this cane into four equal segments.

6 To make the very center of the poppy, create a light green

cylinder about ½ inch in diameter and the same height as the petals. Cut the whole thing in half like a cake and add a brown clay strip about ½ inch thick. Reassemble the halves. Do this one more time then cut the whole thing in half again and add the brown clay.

7 Before you resassemble the piece, insert a thin roll of brown clay as shown; it might help to use a wooden stick to create a depression for this roll. Now reassemble the halves.

8 Wrap the cane in a piece of brown clay about ½ inch thick. Attach a thin half-circle of brown clay to the side of the cane to create the slightly off-center appearance of a real poppy.

9 Now arrange all the parts of the poppy and fill in the spaces between the petals with pieces of a cylinder of translucent clay cut in four.

10 Make two small valleys along the tip of each petal then fill these with very thin rolls of translucent clay. Reduce the entire cane as desired.

• Alternate complex flower cane

Here the petals are made with stacked sheets that form lines surrounding target-style canes.

1 Make a shaded sheet of clay, dark tint to light tint, and place it on a dark rectangular sheet. Place this on another light sheet and place this on a third sheet of a medium tint. Cut this mille-fiori block lengthwise into two equal parts.

2 Wrap a thin roll of color with a white sheet and reduce to create a very thin cane. Cut this into four equal parts then place them on the shaded side of one half of the block, as shown.

3 Fill in the spaces between the rolls with rectangles of color or translucent clay then place the second half of the block on top of the whole thing, keeping the shaded side next to the rolls. Pinch the ends and reduce the cane.

4 Cut the cane into six equal parts and arrange the flower shape. Create a center roll of dark clay wrapped in light clay. Fill in the spaces between the petals with colored or translucent clay.

5 Reduce the cane to the desired size.

• Translucent clay

Translucent clay varies greatly from brand to brand. It might take some experimenting to get the look you want from a particular brand. But the work is worth it. When you work with translucent clay, cut very thin slices: The thicker the slice, the more the clay tends to become opaque. To accentuate the translucency of beads made with this material, drop them into fresh ice-water as soon as they come out of the oven.

Translucent clay is often used to fill in the empty spaces during the creation of the cane.

Don't forget that translucent clay is white before baking and reveals its translucency only after cooling completely. Like other clays, it can be tinted with powders, alcoholic inks, or oil paints.

Using canes

• Charms from cane pieces

A slice of cane about 1/8 inch thick can be used to make a dainty charm. Cut the slice very carefully and bake it flat. In order to avoid deforming it, pierce it after baking by turning a drill between two fingers.

• Sheets

Making a patterned sheet

This kind of sheet allows you lots of flexibility to create unique and stylish projects. It uses a certain number of patterned canes, in assorted or contrasting tones, to create the desired effect.

Composing with sheets

Sheets can be made up of slices of cane scattered randomly, or the pieces can be arranged in a more composed fashion to make little pictures.

Tips for making complex canes

- For canes with complex patterns, use a base pattern with a diameter of at least 2 inches and a thickness of at least $3/4$ inch. Smaller than this and you risk deforming the pattern when you reduce the cane.
- Don't mix clays of different brands (and remember that gold of any brand is often very soft and has a tendency to deform more than other colors).
- To limit the deformation of a pattern, make the base pattern in a definitive shape: round for a round cane, square for a square cane, and so on.
- Keep strong colors separate, with thin layers of white or black between them. This helps prevent the mixing of the colors during baking. Do the same thing to accentuate contrasts: Wrap light colors in black; wrap dark colors in white.
- Bake an extra slice of your came to keep as a model for future projects.
- Make three sizes to create depth or make a complex, harmonious composition.

- Follow a model: printed fabric, a photo, or drawing. If the model is too complicated, simplify it, adjusting the colors as needed.
- Work cleanly, cutting cane borders as precisely as possible. Keep all leftovers, organizing them by color. They can be used to make pretty marbled pieces or new, interesting colors.

- Don't throw scraps away. If you don't like a scrap's color, use it in another mix or as a piece or round bead that will get covered by another color. You can also use it to make molds.
- A simple pattern or a cane that you rarely use could become the basis for a complex or geometric cane. Create your canes with confidence in your creativity.
- It's not always easy to cut a slice of cane without deforming the pattern. If this happens, you can usually stretch it back into shape. Work as gently as possible.
- To limit deformations, let your cane cool down for at least one day before using. This length of time can be reduced by several hours if you put the cane in the refrigerator.
- Thin canes will warm up and soften more quickly than thicker canes will.
- A slice that is too thick can be remodeled with a blade, needle, or tool with a round end and applied as a raised pattern on a surface (see the project on page 128).
- After reduction, canes can sometimes get lightly dented. This doesn't have much impact on the pattern, but, if you want a very even and round cane, polish it by placing a sheet of glass or Plexiglas on it and going over it with a roller.
- When you make a complex pattern, the first parts you make have time to cool down, which will make them firmer than the parts made later. To prevent as much deformation as possible during reduction, the entire piece should have a homogeneous texture and temperature. Let all the parts rest for a while before assembling and then reduce.
- To finish a cane, you will often need to fill the spaces around a pattern to get an even section (a circle, square, or triangle, for example). Translucent clay works best for this, as it complements almost any other color and will allow the cane to be used for a variety of projects.

Working with
Textures

A beach look

Textured on the back and decorated with stamps on the front, this is an easy-to-make necklace for beginners.

Materials for the beads

- One block of white clay
- Fine table salt
- Various stamps
- Round cookie cutter, ½-inch diameter
- Round cookie cutter, 1½-inch diameter
- Drill, 5⁄64-inch bit

Materials for assembly

The necklace
- Off-white novelty "eyelash" yarn, 8 feet
- Eight 10mm frosted glass crystal beads

The earrings
- Two headpins with flower-shaped heads
- Two silver earring studs with pierced metal disks

Making the beads

1 Use a clay machine or roller to prepare a slab of white clay ⅛ inch thick. Fold it in half lengthwise, squeezing out the air bubbles with a roller or rolling pin.

2 Completely cover one of the surfaces with fine salt; push the salt into the clay by pressing a piece of glass on the surface. Then turn the clay over. A

 ADVICE

Turn the slab of clay over with the salt side next to the surface of the plate or tile you'll use when baking. This will prevent you from having to move the beads once they are in their final shape. Clean your work surface to keep from getting salt on other pieces.

3 On the smooth side of the clay, make imprints with the stamps (B) and cut out seven circles 1½ inches in diameter. Cut out the centers of four of the circles with the small cookie cutter (or the cap of a large felt-tipped pen). Bake the circles according to the instructions on the package of clay. C

ADVICE

If the cap of the marker you use has holes in it, so much the better; you can blow into it to help remove the cut piece without damaging it. And you can use the scraps of salty clay for the necklace project on page 53.

Finishing the beads

1 After taking them from the oven, let your beads soak in water to dissolve the salt then brush them if necessary with a toothbrush. D

2 Sand the edges of the beads gently with 600-grit paper, followed by 1000-grit. Also sand any parts of the beads that are not pure white.

3 Use the drill to make a hole in the center of all the little beads, and at ¹/₂ inch from the edges of the three big disks. Leave the four rings as they are.

Assembling the necklace

1 Begin the necklace by cutting the yarn in half and folding each piece in two. Attach them each to one of the full discs as shown. This will be the center disk. E

2 String the beads following the pattern (F), making knots in the yarn between the beads (as indicated by the Ns).

3 Tie a final knot with all four strands to make the necklace your desired length and trim the excess.

✳ ADVICE

Before assembly, place your beads so that the imprinted sides are all facing the same way. You could also put the little ones it the centers of the rings the other way; this will create a subtly contrasting effect.

The earrings

1 Drill each disk with a ⁵/₆₄-inch bit. On the headpin, slide on the metal disks, then the polymer beads.

2 At the back, bend the stem at a 90-degree angle and finish with an earring loop.

✳ ADVICE

You can also use stud backings on the earrings, gluing them with a two-part epoxy cement.

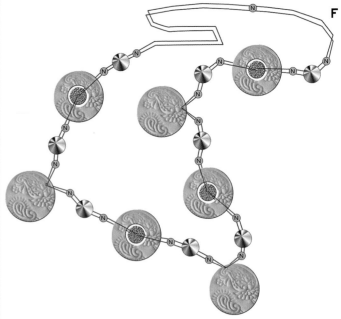

VARIATIONS

This necklace can be made with beads of other shapes or with clay of another color. You can also mix different colors for an interesting effect.

A dramatic look

A bold assembly of stamped pieces finished with acrylic paint and an assortment of interesting beads.

Materials for the beads

- Two blocks of black clay
- Stamp
- White acrylic paint
- Drill, 5/64-inch bit
- Square cookie cutter, 3/4 inch on each side
- Varnish

Materials for assembly

The necklace

- 20-gauge wire, 18 inches
- One two-ring clasp
- One eyepin, 2¾ inches
- One eyepin, 1½ inches
- One headpin
- Black seed beads
- Eighteen opaque crystal bicone beads
- Thirteen round metal 3mm beads
- Two round metal 4mm beads
- Glue

The ring

- One ring base with a flat surface
- Crystal resin
- Two-part epoxy cement

Making the flat beads

1 Prepare a slab of clay 1/8 inch thick and fold it in two lengthwise, taking care to squeeze out air bubbles with a clay roller.
2 Stamp the slab, making eight or so impressions. A

> ### ✿ ADVICE
> *If an air bubble forms between two layers of clay, poke it with the point of a needle and roll over it again. If you leave it there, it may expand during baking and weaken the piece.*

3 Cut pairs of beads, all ³/4 inch wide: two long ones (2 inches long), two medium ones (1½ inches), and two short ones (1 inch). Also cut four squares, ³/4 inch on each side. B
4 Bake the beads, following the manufacturer's instructions.

5 To make holes in these beads, mark the hole position—on both sides of the piece near the top—with the point of a needle immediately after baking. When the bead has cooled, drill one side, stopping halfway then do the same on the other side. Be careful to drill the holes so they are centered and meet precisely.

> ### ✿ ADVICE
> *For this kind of bead, it's better to make the holes after the beads are hard. In unhardened clay, you risk altering the shape of the design on the beads when you pierce them. If you cannot wait, however, at least put your beads in the freezer for a few minutes, and pierce them while they are still on the baking surface.*

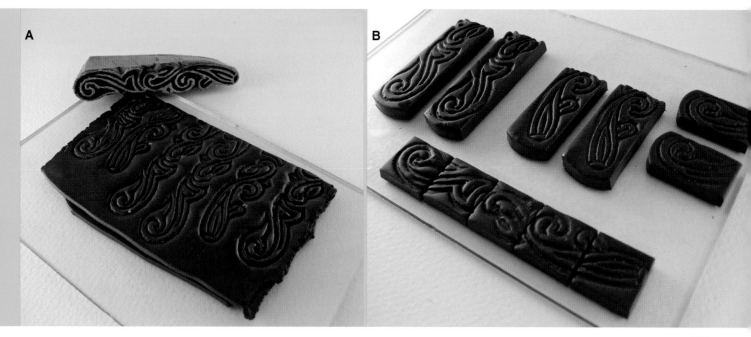

A

B

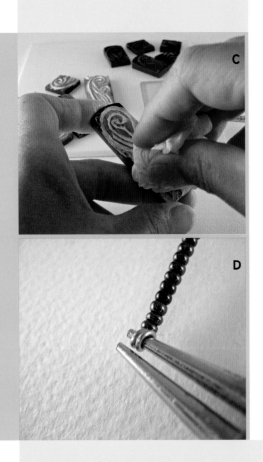

C

D

E

6 Apply white acrylic paint to the surface of the pattern, taking care to get it into all the hollows. Wipe off the excess with a paper towel and let the beads dry completely. C

7 With a piece of wet sandpaper, sand the edges and the backs of the beads as well as the surfaces to allow the black to show through, creating a dramatic contrast with the white patterns.

8 Apply a coat of varnish.

Making the round beads

1 Rub black clay between your thumb and index finger. Press hard to create little flecks of clay.

2 Place the clay flecks into a container and add a small dollop of white acrylic paint.

3 Stir the mixture gently with a small stick, such as a wooden matchstick.

4 Shape the mixture with your fingers into four little balls. The mixture should be more clay than paint.

5 Bake the round beads then sand them to remove paint from the black clay and create an interesting pattern of black and white.

6 Drill the holes before or after baking, as your prefer. Finish with a coat of varnish.

Assembling the necklace

1 The necklace is mounted on 20-gauge wire, which allows it to hold its shape. Make a loop to attach the clasp with a ring on one side and the extension chain on the other. D

2 String on the beads, following the pattern. E

✿ ADVICE

If the beads of the central pendant tend to turn because their holes are a bit too large, use a small drop of glue in the holes to keep them in position.

The ring

1 To make the ring's bead, use the same method as for the flat beads and cut out a square with the cookie cutter. Bake the clay, give it a patina of white acrylic paint, and sand.

2 Prepare the resin and cover the bead with a generous coat. Let it dry for twenty-four hours, protected from dust.

3 Sand the edges again so they are perfectly smooth. Glue the bead onto the ring with epoxy.

✿ ADVICE

For this kind of polymer ring, it's best to not attach the ring until after the resin has dried completely. In fact, the ring will hinder the application of the resin, making it difficult to get the resin to dry completely flat.

A bohemian look

Crackled gold foil on the back, stamps and two-color metallic effects on the front—irresistible charm.

Materials for the beads

- One block of khaki green clay
- Gold foil
- Two different stamps
- Green and gold metallic powder
- Round cookie cutters: 1 inch, ¾ inch, ½ inch in diameter.
- Resin (optional)
- Varnish
- Drill, ⁵⁄₆₄-inch bit

Materials for assembly

The necklace

- Chains, 16 and 18 inches long
- Thirty-eight 7mm rings for the drop beads and two for the clasp
- Green 4mm seed beads
- One snap clasp

The bracelet (see page 41)

- Chain, 7 inches long
- Twelve rings 7mm in diameter for the drop beads and two for the clasp
- One big snap clasp
- Six 4mm bicone beads of green tourmaline crystal
- Three 8mm round light green pearly beads
- Three 8mm round green pearly beads
- Twelve 4mm metal beads
- Six 4mm metal bead caps
- Six 1½ inch headpins

Making the beads

1 With half a block of clay, roll out a sheet ⅛ inch thick then lay a sheet of gold foil on top. Squeeze out air bubbles with your fingertips, being careful not to indent the clay.

2 To get the crackled effect, pass the sheet through the clay machine set at about ⅛ inch. Adjust the setting to go slightly smaller, turn the sheet a quarter turn, and run it through again. Changing the direction gives you both vertical and horizontal crackles. A and B

If you are using a roller, roll out the clay vertically first, then horizontally, until you get little gold squares surrounded by the background clay color.

3 The crackled sheet is for the back of the drop beads; place it directly on the baking surface, foil side down.

4 Roll out a second sheet a little less than ⅛ inch thick and put it on top of the first, squeezing out air bubbles with a roller.

Wear a face mask to protect yourself from the powder, which can be very volatile. Choose a stamp and apply a little gold powder to the raised part. C

5 Stamp the clay with the powdered stamp.

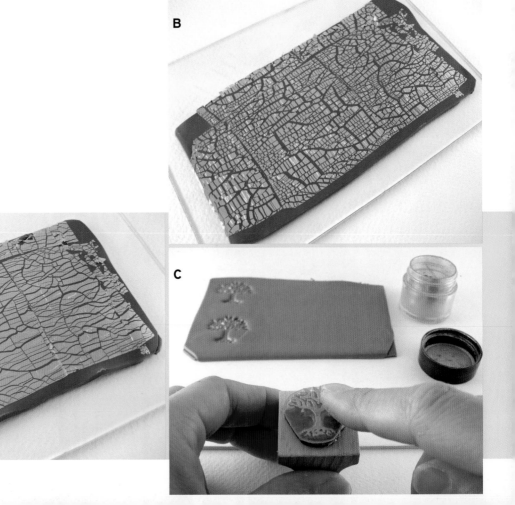

5 Cut out the drop beads with a cookie cutter, taking care to keep the designs centered. For the necklace, you'll need three big beads 1 inch in diameter and sixteen medium ones ³⁄₄ inch in diameter. D

6 Apply the green powder, brushing it lightly over the raised parts of the beads. Smooth out any accidental marks you've made—you won't be able to sand these beads.

7 With the remaining clay, roll out a new sheet ¹⁄₈ inch thick and cover the top completely with gold foil. Crackle it as you did previously and fold the resulting sheet in half, foil side out. E and F

8 Cut out nineteen circles ¹⁄₂ inch in diameter (a large pen cap works well for this). Save the leftover clay with the scraps of foil to make the crackle surface of the bracelet. G

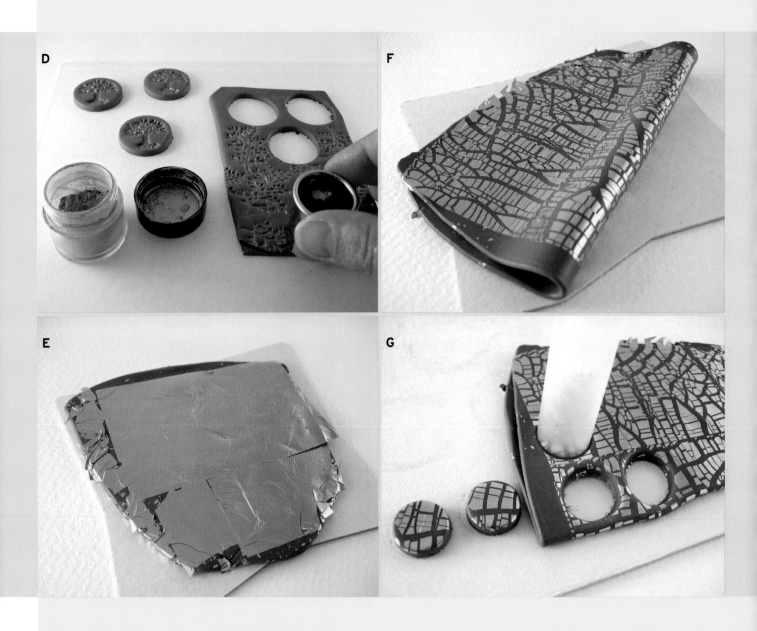

The beads for the bracelet

1 For the bracelet, make four drop beads ³⁄₄ inch in diameter with the crackle surface on one side and stamp motif on the other, and eight drop beads ¹⁄₂ inch in diameter, with the crackle surface on both sides.

✳ ADVICE

If you use Cleopatra brand high-gloss varnish, bake it before sanding the edges of the beads. Remember that this varnish takes a long time to dry completely—as long as a week. Make sure it doesn't get damp during this time; it could become white if it comes into contact with water.

2 Apply a coat of varnish on both sides to protect the powder and foil.
3 Sand the edges of the drop beads.
4 Apply another coat of varnish over the whole of the beads and drill holes in them, ¹⁄₈ inch from the edge. Apply resin to the stamped surfaces if you wish.

Assembling the necklace

Join the two chains with a ring, leaving unequal lengths on the two sides, and spread out the beads, putting the small ones in between the large ones. H

Assembling the bracelet

1 Spread out the four medium beads on the chain, mounted on a ring with one seed bead, and place a small polymer bead on each side. I
2 On the headpins, slip on the gold-colored metal, crystal bicone, and round pearly beads. Make three strands with the big light-colored beads and three others with the dark-colored beads. Mount them on the chain with a ring in the gaps and add the clasp.

A retro look

With a pretty patina on both sides, the beads of this necklace have one smooth surface and one textured surface. You can dance without worrying about them flipping over.

Materials for the beads

- Two blocks of black clay
- One block of silver clay
- Two textured sheets with different patterns
- Black and silver acrylic paint
- Flower-shaped cookie cutter (at least 1½ inch in diameter)
- The cap of a large marker, ½ inch in diameter
- Varnish
- Drill, ³⁄₆₄-inch bit (necklace)
- Drill, ⁵⁄₆₄-inch bit (charm)
- Ten ½-inch eyepins

Materials for assembly

The necklace

- Three links with two loops
- Five unbroken rings, 1¼-inch diameter
- Four unbroken rings, ½-inch diameter
- Eight round filigree flowers, 1½-inch diameter
- Chain, 4 inches
- Five 2¾-inch eyepins
- Six 6mm round faceted beads
- Five 10mm round frosted class crystal beads
- Ten 2mm black seed beads
- Forty 7mm rings
- Superglue

The charm

- One large lobster-claw clasp
- Black organza ribbon, 20 inches, ¼ inch thick
- Patterned ribbon, 4 inches
- Four round ½-inch filigree flowers
- Three links with two loops
- Nine 7mm rings
- Glue

Making the beads

1 Make a ball of black clay ¾ inch in diameter and flatten it between two smooth surfaces to create a disk 1¼ inch wide. Make as many disks as desired (five are used in this project). A

2 Make a sheet of silver clay ⅛ inch thick and print it with a textured sheet. Make sure the surface is big enough to cover all the beads you just made.

3 Mix the black and silver paint then apply it to the textured clay. Wipe the paint off the raised parts with a paper towel and let it dry. B

4 Use the flower-shaped cutter to cut out as many shapes as you need for both sides of the disks. Apply them to both sides of the disks, folding all the petals down over the edges. C

5 Cut holes in the centers with the marker lid and gently smooth both sides of the disks with a wet pane of glass or Plexiglas, as shown. D

6 Make five other beads the same way-but use a textured sheet with a different pattern and skip the step in which you cut out the centers.

✳ ADVICE
Take half of the mold off and trim the excess clay with a cookie cutter while the piece is still on the baking surface. Gently detach the shaped clay, without marring any of the details.

Finishing the beads

1 Bake the beads according to the manufacturer's instructions.

2 Before applying a patina, sand the edges of each bead.

3 If you use an acrylic patina finish, you might want to apply a coat of varnish after it dries.

Assembling the necklace

1 With your smallest drill bit, make holes in the "solid" beads 1/2 inch from each side then glue in the eyepins. E

2 Drill holes in the "centerless" beads from one side to the other. You can make these holes before baking, but you risk bending the beads out of shape if you do.

3 Set a round frosted glass bead in the centers of the two hollow beads and a seed bead on each side. Then set the

G

H

I

five others with the same beads in the middle and a round faceted bead on each side. Close up the eyepin with a loop that matches the one at the head. F

Then follow the pattern. G

✱ADVICE

To make the second hole in line with the first, put a needle through the first hole and adjust your movement as needed.

Assembling the charm

1 Drill holes in your two beads ¼ inch from the edge. Thread the ribbon through the clasp, fold it in two, and knot the two strands together. Make a second knot ¾ inch farther down. Pass the end of one ribbon through the bead with the help of a fine wire folded in half (acting as a needle) then thread the other ribbon through in the opposite direction. H

2 Make a loop knot with the two remaining ends of ribbon and add a drop of glue for a good hold. Do the same thing with the second clay bead, extending the ribbons a bit to separate the two beads.

3 Fold the fancy ribbon in half through the clasp and attach it with a very tight ring. Attach three filigree flowers to the links and link them to the clasp with a ring. Slide the ring directly through the last flower. I

A sophisticated look

A unique texture and acrylic patina give this simple piece a sophisticated look.

Materials for the beads

- Black, burgundy, orange, and beige clay
- Liquid Fimo clay
- Copper metallic powder
- Black acrylic paint, inkpad, and ink roller
- Mini cookie press in the shape of a flower
- Oval cookie cutter, about ¾ inch by 1 ⅛ inches
- Stamp
- Piece of lace with a raised pattern
- Gedeo crystal resin or Kato Polyclay

Materials for assembly

The necklace (see page 49)

- One velvet choker
- One screw-in hook, ½ inch long, with the ring ¼ inch in diameter

The pin

- One glue-on pin back, 1 ½ inches long

Making the textured sheet

1 Take a piece of lace and lay it very flat, with its face against a ⅛-inch thick sheet of scrap clay

2 Put the lace and clay through the clay machine set to ⅛ inch then place the clay sheet on a piece of glass or ceramic surface. Carefully remove the lace. Trim the edges without marring the texture.

3 Bake the clay. (You can now reuse this textured sheet many times.)

✳**ADVICE**

To keep the sheet from losing its shape in the oven, press if to the glass or ceramic, squeezing out any air bubbles. A sheet of glass is best suited for this. Don't bake this sheet on parchment paper, as larger clay sheets have a tendency to bulge on this, which makes the sheet very difficult to use. After baking, let the sheet cool on the glass.

The plate for the pendant

1 Cut a rectangle 1¼ inch by 3 inches from an ⅛-inch-thick sheet of black clay. This will be the base of the pendant.

2 Make a shaded sheet of clay that goes from burgundy to orange (see page 15 for instructions).

3 In order to easily detach a textured sheet from the clay, spray a little water on the mold, or brush on a little bit of talcum powder with a paintbrush; the powder must not build up in any of the crevices of the mold, as this will mar the clay. Press the textured sheet into the shaded clay then carefully remove it. Put the sheet in the freezer for a few minutes so you don't crush the design while working with it. A

4 From the shaded sheet, choose an interesting area and cut out a ¾ by 3 inch rectangle. Put this on the black base so a black strip along one side is left uncovered.

A

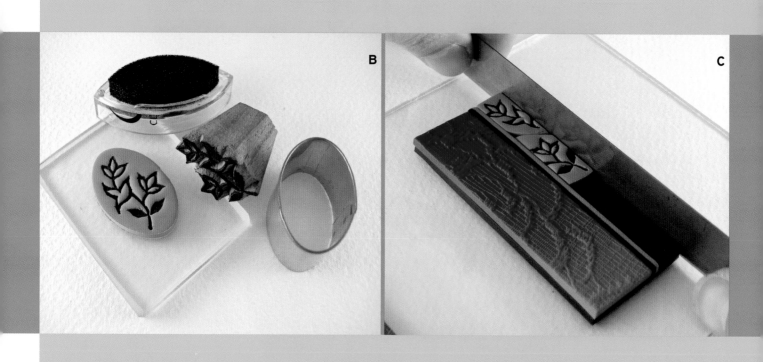

B

C

5 Mix one part of the remaining shaded clay and one part of the beige to get a salmon pink tone and set aside a bit of this (enough to accommodate the oval cookie cutter). With the rest of the pink clay, make a sheet ⅛ inch thick. Make a same-size same sheet from black clay and place the pink on top then run it through the clay machine. You want to create a strip at least 3 inches long. From this, cut out strips ⅛ inch wide.

6 Take one of these strips and place it on its side, along the length of the lace-textured rectangle. Adhere it by pressing it with the side of a knife blade.

7 With the salmon clay you set aside, make a small disk and apply a stamp inked in black. Cut around the design with the oval cookie cutter and let it dry. B

8 Cut the stamped oval in two pieces, however you like, and arrange the pieces at the upper right of the lace print on the black base clay. Press them in with a blade. The gaps will be filled later. C

9 With the mini cookie press, make three beige flowers from a sheet of clay and place them on the black base sheet.

10 Fill in the space between the flowers with bits of the two-colored strips then trim the edges neatly. D

11 Cut another two-color strip a little higher than the others (2 inches long) and apply it to the edge of the sheet, black edge out. Use a blade to finish the border on the right.

Finish the other three edges of the pendant with a strip of black ½ inch thick, trimming neatly at the corners.

12 Tint a bit of liquid Fimo with metallic powder and fill in the gaps in the piece. Bake the whole piece. E

❋ **ADVICE**

To get the flowers easily out of the cookie cutter without using a press, which can leave marks, stick the clay onto a sheet of glass. The flowers will stay attached to the glass, and you can take them off by sliding a thin blade underneath.

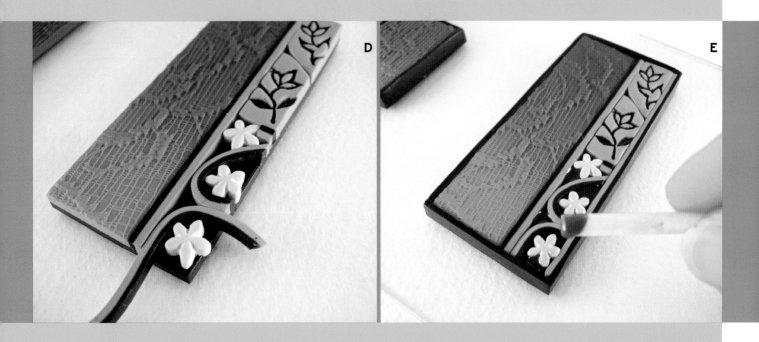

Finishing

1 Apply a patina of black acrylic paint to the raised lace surface with a paper towel then let it dry.

2 Sand the flowers then apply a coat of Kato Polyclay, hardening it with a heat gun. For a smoother effect, apply a second coat (a coat of Gedeo crystal resin can be used instead). Let it dry for at least a day, protected from dust.

3 Sand the edges and make a hole where the hook should go.

The pin

1 Work with a sheet of black clay $1^{1}/_{4}$ inch by $1^{1}/_{4}$ inch; add a textured rectangle $1^{1}/_{4}$ by 1 inch. Proceed as you did for the pendant.

2 When the clay is baked, mark the placement of the pin back with the point of a knife. Glue on the back with liquid polymer; cover with a rectangle of black clay $1^{1}/_{8}$ inches by $^{1}/_{2}$ inch, with the metallic part in contact with the black sheet.

3 Bake it again. Sand and apply a coat of resin.

✸ ADVICE

It's important that the paint covers only the raised parts of the lace pattern and not the crevices. To do this, put only a little bit of paint in a container and wipe off your paper-towel swab well before lightly brushing the relief. Take your time, applying the paint sparingly.

An antique look

Textures and patinas give these pieces the appearance of ancient Roman coins.

Materials for the beads

- Two blocks of black clay
- One textured button
- One round cookie cutter, ¾-inch diameter
- One round cookie cutter, 1¼-inch diameter
- Gold paint
- Bright aqua acrylic paint
- Glue
- Toothpick
- Varnish

Materials for assembly

The necklace (see page 52)

- Black 2mm seed beads
- Fifty-two 4mm bohemian glass faceted beads
- Six 6mm faceted bohemian glass beads
- One 10mm bohemian glass bead (for the clasp)
- Jewelry wire, 20 inches
- Two crimp beads
- Nylon thread, 20 inches, 0.25mm thick
- Jewelry glue
- Drill, 3⁄64-inch bit

Making the beads

1 In a sheet of black clay ⅛ inch thick, cut out thirteen circles, each 1¼ inch in diameter. Roll them into balls and place them on a sheet of glass or ceramic tile.

2 Moisten the button with water and press it into the balls of clay. Press so that the clay spreads out all around the button then carefully pull it out. Try to make each piece the same. A

3 Cut off the edges of each piece with the ¾-inch cookie cutter (the exact size depends on the button you use).

4 In a black sheet of clay 1⁄16 inch thick, cut thirteen rectangles ½ inch by 1 inch. Roll up a toothpick in each halfway as shown and do the same on the other side. Press lightly to make the two tubes stick together without deforming them. The wire will go through these tubes.

5 In a sheet of black clay ⅛ inch thick, cut thirteen circles 1 inch in diameter, directly on the baking surface.

6 Attach the double tube, flat side up, to the upper half of the circles. Press the tubes lightly with a wet sheet of glass to make sure they stick. Gently twist the toothpicks and pull them out of the clay. B

7 Bake all the pieces then sand carefully, using 1500-grit paper, followed by 2000-grit paper.

8 Patina the textured disks in two steps. First, apply a coat of aqua paint, making sure all the crevices are filled, and wipe off the excess with a paper towel.

9 Then lightly brush the raised parts with the gold paint, using a piece of paper towel.

10 Let the pieces dry then apply a coat of varnish. Glue the textured disks to the center of the plain black beads. Polish the black surfaces (I use my drill with a bit of lambskin attached to the bit).

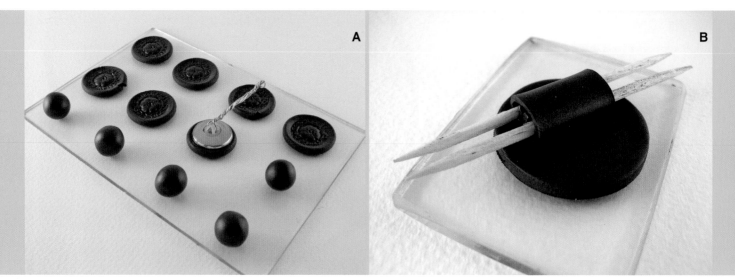

Assembling the necklace

1 On the first six beads, make one hole just to the right of the tube's opening (if the bead is held so that the rolled tube is at the top), using your drill. On the six other beads, make a hole on the left. These holes are for the nylon thread, used to keep the beads in place. Leave the thirteenth bead unpierced; this will be the central bead.

2 Begin assembling the necklace at the center of the jewelry wire, which you should fold in half. Make a loop with twenty-five seed beads. Then insert ten seed beads and one round 6mm bead, passing both wires through them. Repeat this twice then separate the wires and put five seed beads and a 4mm bohemian bead on each wire. C

3 Work with the necklace upside-down. Begin stringing the clay beads that have the holes on the right. Put the wires through the two tubes and add two 4mm faceted beads before the next clay bead.

4 As you string the beads on the wire, run the nylon thread through the lower tube and then through the hole. It will come out on the front of the clay. The nylon doesn't go through the faceted beads; it goes directly into the next tube, always through the lower one. As a result, the beads will overlap nicely, like stairs.

5 Proceed with the six clay beads with holes on the right.

6 Place the center bead and thread through the wires and the nylon. D

7 Continue stringing with the beads that have holes on the left to finish your necklace symmetrically. Instead of a loop at the end, use the 10mm round bead, attached between two crimp beads.

8 Trim the wires. E

9 Take up the nylon and bring it back toward the beginning of the necklace, passing it through the tubes on top.

10 When the thread comes through the last tube, knot it and apply a drop of glue to the knot. You can hide this with a 4mm faceted bead. Now trim the thread.

11 You can, of course, adjust the number of beads depending on how long you want the necklace to be.

An authentic look

Texturing and creating effects with tinted liquid polymer clay
is a great way to create translucency.

✳ ADVICE
*This project can be made using the leftover clay
mixed with salt from the project on page 32.
Add more salt to create a grainier texture.*

Materials for the beads

- One block of white clay
- Fine salt
- Liquid Fimo clay
- Green alcohol ink
- Various stamps
- Varnish
- Palette knife (or other flat blade)
- Cookie cutters, 1 ¼ inches, ¾ inch,
  ¼ inch in diameter

Materials for assembly

- 16-gauge brass wire, 16 inches
- Three 4mm round metal beads
- One 2mm round metal bead
- One 8mm round peridot green crystal bead
- One 6mm peridot crystal butterfly
- One metal charm-holder bead
- Four decorated unbroken metal rings,
  ¼-inch diameter
- Two finishing cones in worked metal
- One magnet clasp and two rings
- Two eyepins and one round-tipped headpin
- Green metallic organza tube ribbon, 7 feet
- Drill, ³⁄₆₄-inch bit

Making the necklace beads

The round beads

1 Make six round beads in three sizes and three different shades (see page 16): two 14mm beads in a dark shade, two 12mm beads in a medium shade, and two 10mm beads in a light shade.

2 Make holes in the beads big enough for the brass wire to go through.

3 Bake the pieces following the manufacturer's instructions. Leave them unpolished.

The ceramic faces

1 Mix the white clay and salt well to create a grainy consistency. Make two thin sheets of the salty clay and place them on the top and bottom of a ⅛ inch sheet of unsalted clay.

2 Place the clay on the baking surface and roll the sheet by hand to squeeze out air bubbles.

3 Make three stamps in the clay, leaving some space in between each. A

4 Use cookie cutters to cut the clay, centering the motif of the stamp in three circles: one 1¼ inches in diameter, one ¾ inch in diameter, and one ¼ inch in diameter. B

5 Mix a bit of liquid clay with alcohol ink of the desired color. Using a palette knife, cover the beads with a thin coat of this clay, making certain that the design is still visible. C

✳ ADVICE
*With the tip of a needle, you can lightly
"weather" the texture of the pieces, adding
some streaks near the edges and a few tiny
holes.*

6 Bake the pieces, following the manufacturer's instructions. If you aren't satisfied with the result, you can apply another layer of liquid clay and bake them again.

7 Drill holes through the centers of the beads, going side to side.

Finishing the beads

1 Let the beads soak in lukewarm water until the salt is completely dissolved. If necessary, brush the beads with a toothbrush. It's important to get all the salt off the surface, otherwise it can become sticky when damp and prematurely wear your finish.

2 Very lightly sand the border and bottom of the bead with 600-grit paper.

3 Apply a coat of varnish to the faces.

✳ ADVICE

For a different effect, the surface can be varnished with a crackling medium, which is sold under a variety of brands. Once dry, apply a patina with a shade slightly darker than the one you used for the beads.

Assembling the necklace

1 Thread the metallic organza onto a piece of brass wire cut to the length desired for the choker then attach it at one end by wrapping it firmly with fine wire. Close up the ends of the metal cone to hide this fastening, pushing it inside the cone.

2 Make the loop for the clasp of the choker to hold the fastening in place and so you can begin stringing the beads.

3 Start by stringing on one small round bead–on the wire but on the inside of the ribbon.

4 String on the decorative ring, passing the ribbon and the wire through it.

5 Continue with one medium bead inside the ribbon, then one ring on the outside, and so on, taking care to place the charmholder bead between the two 14mm beads. Assemble all the way around the neck in a symmetrical fashion; adjust the materials as you go, spreading out the ruffles evenly.

6 Make the central pendant with the eyepins, following the pattern. E and F

✳ ADVICE

If the beads of the central pendant have a tendency to turn, hold them in place on the pin with a drop of glue.

D

E

F

54

A Mediterranean look

A subtle combination of textures and effects using colored liquid clay with metal foil–this project requires several bakings, but the result is worth the effort.

Materials for the watch tiles

- One block of silver clay
- Square cookie cutter, ¾ inch on each side
- Silver metallic foil (the type used for gilding)
- Liquid blue Fimo clay
- Alcohol ink and a small stick
- Silver ink
- White acrylic paint
- Cellophane
- One stamp
- Varnish
- Palette knife

Materials for assembly

The watch
- Clear elastic thread, 0.8 mm in diameter, 16 inches
- One rectangular or square watch face
- Four 4mm metal beads
- Sixteen 4mm blue crystal bicone beads
- Eight 4mm cube-shaped crystal AB beads
- Jewelry glue

The earrings
- Two earring attachments
- Eight 5mm rings
- Four eyepins
- Four 4mm blue crystal bicones
- Two 4mm cube-shaped crystal AB beads
- Two 6mm cube-shaped crystal AB beads
- Four 4mm round metal beads
- Eighteen silver seed beads

First baking of the tiles

1 Make a clay sheet ⅛ inch thick and apply the metal foil, tone on tone: gold on gold clay, copper on copper clay, or, as here, silver on silver clay. Smooth it out well with your finger or with the side of a blade to squeeze out any air bubbles. A

Make prints with the stamp on the sheet of clay, taking care not to damage the foil.
2 Put the clay on the baking surface (if it's not already there). Cut out the shapes with a cookie cutter: six flat square tiles, ¾ inch on each side. Bake these shapes, following the manufacturer's instructions. C

As soon as the clay comes out of the oven, gently scrap off the foil covering all the edges, being careful not to damage the surface.

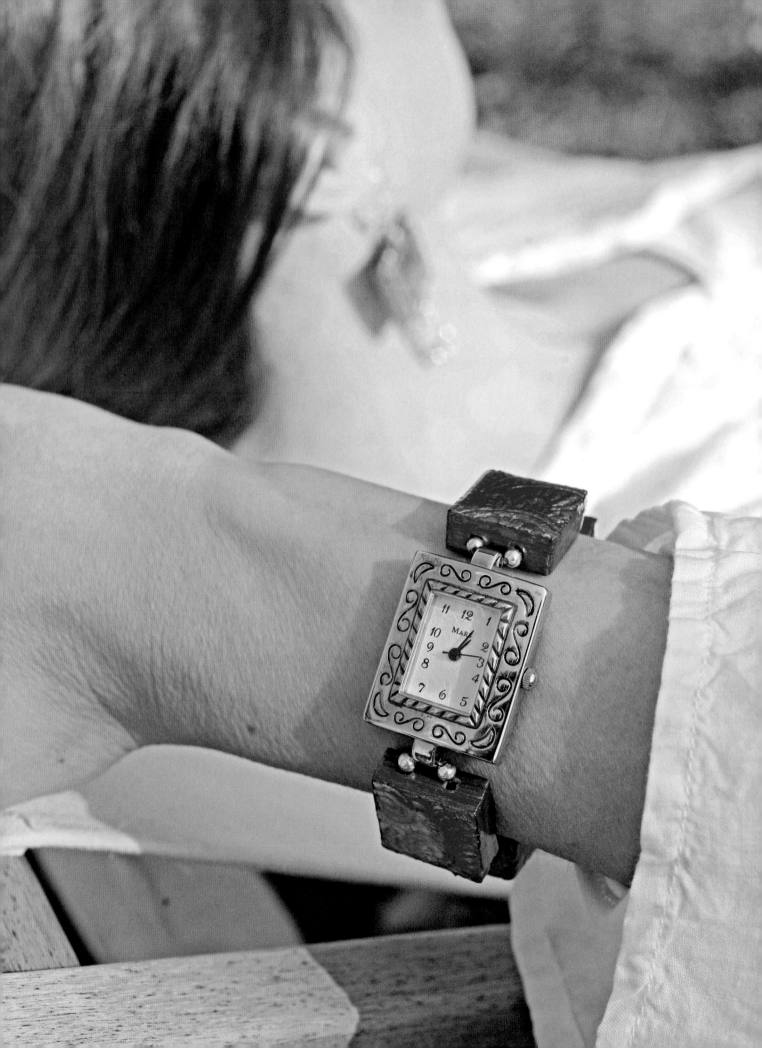

Second baking of the tiles

1 Make a base sheet $1/16$ inch thick from silver clay—this sheet must be big enough for all the tiles to fit on it. Make a second identical sheet to be used as support and place it on a baking surface (writing paper will work well).

2 On the first sheet, trace the outline of all the tiles in the clay, adding two parallel channels through which jewelry wire will pass (as seen in photo D).

3 Place this sheet on a piece of cellophane and make it stick. Cut out the shapes of the tiles, along with the channels for the wire, without moving the rest.

4 Place the clay that's on the cellophane face down on the second clay sheet that's affixed to the baking surface. Roll the back of the cellophane lightly with a hand roller so clay sticks to clay. Gently pull away the cellophane.

5 Cut the squares out again with the cookie cutter to create square tiles with channels on the backs. Apply a thin coat of liquid polymer clay with a paintbrush, taking care not to fill in the channels. Affix the hardened tiles you made before, pressing them firmly onto the clay without deforming the base. D

6 In a small container, mix a little liquid polymer with a few drops of alcohol ink (the more ink you put in, the darker a color you will get). Mix well with a small stick, being careful to avoid making bubbles.

7 Apply the colored mixture to the tiles in a fine coat. If it's too thick, it might run when it's heated, which will obscure the patterns. Be careful not to move the tiles during this process; they will not really be held together by the liquid polymer until they are hard. Bake the pieces, following the manufacturer's instructions.

❋ADVICE
Set aside one paintbrush for applying liquid clay. You just need to wipe it off after use and protect it from dust by placing its tip in a small plastic bag or by washing it with soapy water. Then it will always be ready when you need it.

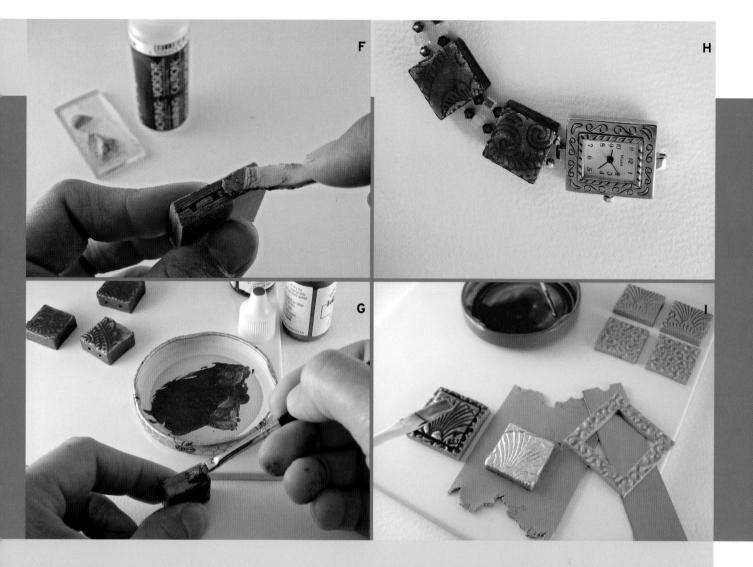

Finishing the beads

1 Gently sand the edges of each bead with 400-grit paper so that you make fine grooves in the clay. But be careful not to mar the colored surface. E

2 Prepare a "filler" by mixing a bit of silver clay with liquid polymer. Using a palette knife, fill in any large cracks or holes on the sides of the tiles—but be careful not to get the filler in the holes made for the wires. F

3 Bake the tiles again then sand the edges with finer sandpaper.

4 Add two drops of blue to silver paint, which will be used to simulate enamel. Apply this color to the edges of the tiles without getting it on the faces. G

Let the beads dry then apply a varnish. A shiny coat will be the prettiest. You can also, if you wish, apply resin.

Assembling the watch

String the beads on a strand of clear elastic thread, starting with the watch face in the middle of the strand. Between each polymer bead and the next, add one small crystal cube placed between two blue bicones.

Finish with a knot strengthened by a drop of jewelry glue. Hide the knot inside the hole of a polymer bead. H

The earrings

Proceed as you did for the watch, making two square tiles 3/4 inch on each side. The tile is then attached to a sheet 1/16 inch thick and a textured frame is added all around it. I

Make one hole in the tile on the upper side to attach the earring and two holes on the lower side to attach the two pendants made of seed and crystal beads strung on a silver round-head pin.

Working with
Different Materials

A natural look

Opaque mokume gane–an interesting technique and a little bit of nature around your neck!

Materials for the beads

- Half a block of khaki green clay
- One block of beige clay
- One stamp
- Round cookie cutters
  (1 ¼ and 1 ½ inches in diameter)
- Drill, ³⁄₃₂-inch bit
- Varnish

Materials for assembly

The necklace

- Waxed cotton cord same color as the beads, 7 feet
- One large crimp bead

The bracelet

- Waxed cotton cord same color as the beads, 7 feet

Making the beads for the necklace

The round beads

1 Make nine round beige beads about 4½ inches in diameter (see page 16).
2 Make holes through the centers, bake, and sand the beads, but don't polish them; you want to keep a matte effect. (You could also use salt beads.)

The flat beads

1 Use the mokume gane technique (see page 21) to combine green and beige clay, creating a sheet.
2 Place the sheet on a piece of paper and smooth it gently with a clay roller.
3 Use the cookie cutters to cut out six smaller disks and one larger disk. Don't remove the disks from the paper.

Finishing the beads

1 Bake the disks following the manufacturer's instructions.
2 Lightly sand the surfaces of the mokume gane pieces with very fine paper–this material is particularly fragile. You can use coarser paper on the edges and the backs, however.
3 Use the drill to make holes in the disks ⅛ inch from the edge. The cotton cord must be able to pass through this hole twice.
4 Apply a coat of varnish to create a shiny appearance.

Assembling the necklace

1 Fold the cord in half and string on a beige bead, holding it in place with a knot. A
2 With the two strands, make a second knot ¾ inch farther down, then a third knot ¾ inch farther from that.
3 On one of the two strands–we'll call it the "front strand"–thread a round bead and hold it in place with a knot tying both strands together. The other strand goes behind the bead. Use a needle to slide the knot right up next to the bead; this will help keep your knots even. B
4 Cross the two strands through the hole in a small flat bead, the front strand entering on the front of the bead. Make a tight knot where they come out and don't leave any space between the bead and the knot; they need to be right up next to each other so the necklace stays even and is held together tightly. C

 ADVICE
To easily cross the cords through the disk, put the first through then use a scrap of wire bent in two to put the other cord through in the opposite direction.

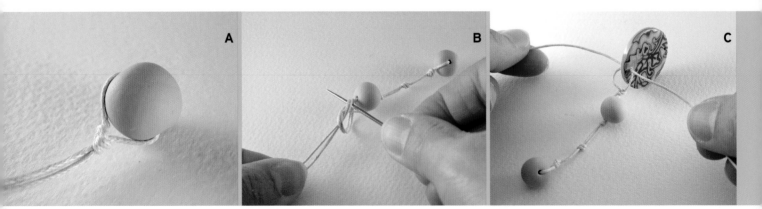

A

B

C

5 Continue in the same fashion, alternating between round beads and disks with crossed strands. Don't forget to knot after every bead you add and put the big flat bead at the center of the necklace.

6 Finish the necklace with a length of cord symmetrical to the other side and knot it, making a loop that can act as a buttonhole. Remember: The loop must be big enough for the round bead to go through it.

7 To keep the ends of the cords from fraying, join them together with a large crimp bead.

Making the beads for the bracelet

1 Use the mokume gane technique to make clay then cut and make five beads as you did for the necklace.

2 Make seven round beige beads identical to those you made for the necklace.

3 Bake the beads according to the manufacturer's instructions.

4 Gently sand and apply a varnish to the mokume gane beads only.

5 Make holes in the beads exactly opposite each other.

❋ **ADVICE**

To make the holes correctly for the bracelet, use a paper template. Cut out a circle the same size as the bead, fold it in half, and mark the placements of the holes on the fold line. Make marks in the clay with the point of a needle using the template as a guide then pierce the clay with the drill.

Assembling the bracelet

1 Begin as you did for the necklace, but reduce the space between the first knots to 1/2 inch. String on round and flat beads, without forgetting the knot between each pair of beads. D

2 After the five flat beads, knot your threads to make a loop adjusted to the size of the round bead serving as the clasp. E

3 Continue by going back through the other holes, adding another round bead in between each pair of flat beads.

4 At the end of the bracelet, fix the strands together and knot the ends, adding a round bead. F

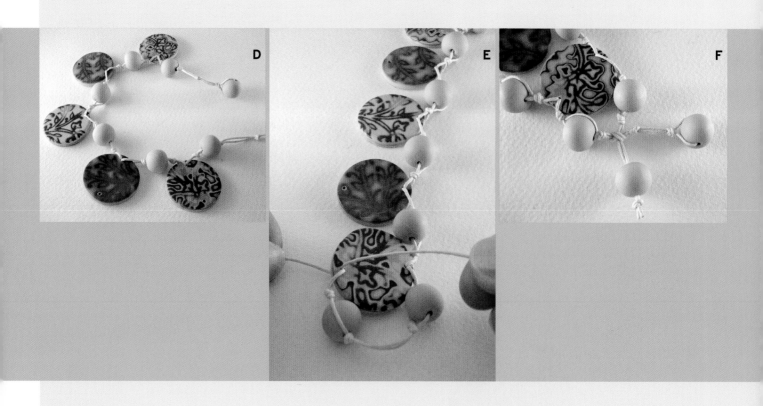

A sparkling look

Metallic foil gives the translucent mokume gane in these beads a little sparkle.

Materials for the mokume gane

- Quarter block of pearly red clay
- An eighth of a block of burgundy clay
- An eighth of a block of beige clay
- Half a block of translucent clay
- Metallic foil

Material for the beads

The necklace

- Half a block of light red clay
- Quarter block of burgundy clay
- Half a block of light-colored clay
  (for the inside of the beads)
- Block of the mokume gane with foil
- Varnish

The bracelet (see page 67)

- Quarter block of burgundy clay
- Pinch of pearly red clay

Materials for assembly

The necklace

- Jewelry wire, three 18-inch lengths
- Sixteen 4mm red crystal bicones
- Mini bronze seed beads
- 2mm bronze seed beads
- 4mm bronze seed beads
- Eighteen 4mm bead caps
- Two crimp beads
- Two bead tips
- Clasp and rings
- Round cookie cutter, ¾-inch diameter
- Two-part crystal resin
- Fine salt
- Nylon thread

The bracelet

- Four round cabochon settings, ¾-inch
  diameter
- Jewelry wire, 24 inches
- Sixteen 4mm red crystal bicones
- Mini bronze seed beads
- 2mm bronze seed beads
- 4mm bronze seed beads
- Six small 4mm bead caps
- Two crimp beads
- Two bead tips
- Bronze-colored clasp and rings
- Flat pliers

Making the mokume gane

1 Make four squares 2 inches on each side and ½ inch thick with a quarter block of pearly red clay.

2 Make two identical squares with the block of burgundy clay, two with the block of beige clay, and eight with the block of translucent clay.

3 Put a sheet of metallic foil on each square and stack them, with every other one a translucent sheet.

Making the beads

The necklace

1 Make the cores of the round beads by cutting disks ¾ inch in diameter from a sheet of light-colored clay ⅛ inch thick. Make twelve beads out of one of these disks of clay and three beads out of four disks of clay. Cover the beads with thin slices of mokume gane and smooth the surfaces. A

2 Make three larger beads and flatten them between two sheets of glass. B

3 In a thick sheet of pearly red clay, cut ten small circles. Shape them into balls then flatten them with the glass. Because these

ADVICE

To emphasize the translucency, put the mokume gane beads into a container of ice water as soon as you take them out of the oven.

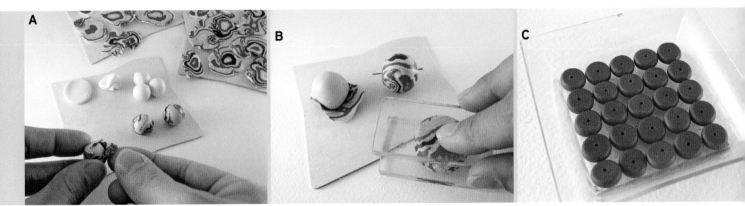

beads are so small, make holes in them before baking. C

4 Make eight salt beads in two different shades of red.

❋ADVICE

Since the mokume gane is made of translucent clay, don't use it to cover scrap clay—the color of the clay underneath will show through, producing an undesirable effect.

The bracelet

1 Make the cabochons by folding a sheet of red 1/8 inch thick in half and place on it the sheets of the mokume gane you've made.

2 Cut four circles 3/4 inch in diameter from each sheet.

3 Bake them according to the manufacturer's instructions.

4 Sand the beads then apply a varnish or resin for a pretty look.

5 Make three burgundy salt beads and two small beads from pearly red.

Assembling the necklace

1 Begin by pinching together the three wires with a crimp bead; hide the crimp in the first bead tip. Continue working by stringing the different-sized seed beads on the three wires, in groups of five or ten, with red bicones between the groupings.

2 String a round mokume gane bead on one strand of wire and a light red salt bead on another, with a small pearly red bead on each one. Put one dark red salt bead on the last strand. The three round clay beads should end up separated.

3 Loosely braid the three strands to create an interesting design.

4 Put all three strands through a large flat bead and continue on the three separate strands, reproducing the set of beads you put on at the beginning but inverting the order.

5 At the center of the necklace, surround the flat bead with two round mokume gane beads and two small pearly red beads and finish the necklace so it is symmetrical.

6 Finish by going through the bead tip then concealing it with a crimp bead. Trim the loose ends of wire.

Assembling the bracelet

1 Fold the wire in half and place a seed bead at the halfway point. Slide the two strands through the hole of a closeable bead tip.

2 Begin working with four seed beads on each strand, then cross the strands through the hole of a little round flat polymer bead. Continue with a big seed bead, a crystal bicone, and three small

seed beads. Thread on a cabochon setting and continue with another three small seed beads, one bicone, and a large seed bead. Cross the strands through a salt bead with a bead cap on each side (D). Continue this way until you have put on the four empty settings and three round salt beads.

3 Finish with three seed beads on each strand–then thread the strands through the bead tip, then through the crimp bead. Fix it in place after you're sure that the beads are all strung as you want them.

4 Put the cabochons in and squeeze the hooks with flat pliers.

5 Attach the clasp to one side and the ring to the other.

❋ADVICE

It's best to attach the clasp through the loop of a mini seed bead with a jump ring and not directly to the wire. That way if it breaks, you just have to change the clasp by opening the ring. To easily thread the wires through the holes in the cabochon settings, put them on without the polymer beads, which you can add at the end of the work.

D

A neon look

Use the unpredictable effects of mokume gane created with a clay gun for this colorful double-length necklace.

Materials for the beads

- One block of scrap clay
- One block of silver clay
- One block of gray clay
- One block of burgundy clay
- One block of green clay
- Clay gun
- One square cookie cutter, ¾ inch on each side (used to make round beads of identical sizes, as explained on page 16)
- Round and square tips for the clay gun

Materials for assembly

The necklace

- Jewelry wire, 5 feet
- Green and amethyst shiny 4mm seed beads
- 8mm miracle beads, in the same shades as the polymer clay beads
- Two crimp beads

The charm (see page 70)

- Five 14mm round beads
- One light pink miracle bead
- Several thin ribbons the same shade as the beads
- Organza ribbon
- One bronze lobster-claw clasp

Making the necklace beads

For this extra-long necklace, you'll make seventeen round beads, about ½ inch in diameter. Mix together different types of beads.

Make a cord of color with the clay gun by placing different clay pieces, one after the other, in the tube. A

Type 1

Wrap the clay cord in a spiral around a ball of scrap clay. You can keep the corded pattern or smooth it out by rolling the ball in your hands. B

Type 2

Use the Type 1 bead and shave it randomly then roll it in your hands so it becomes round again. C

Apply the leftover shavings to a ball to make a matching bead.

You can also apply the shavings upside-down in new positions on the shaved bead. D

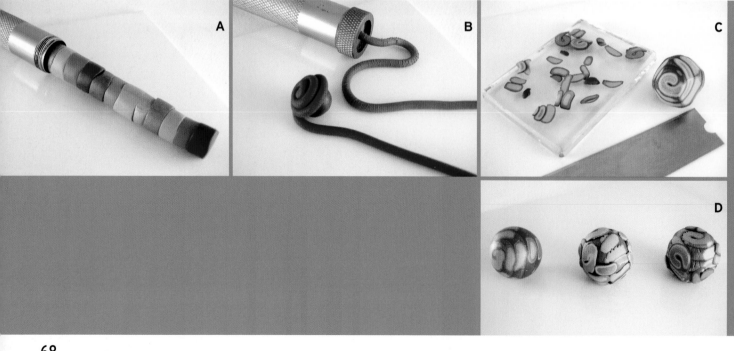

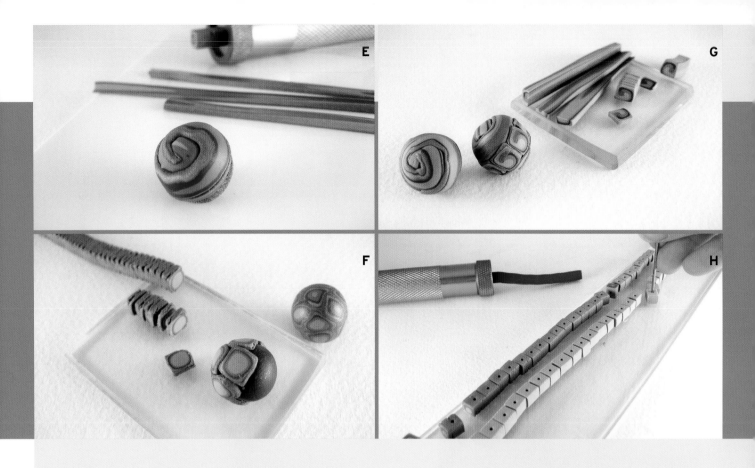

Type 3

Cut a square cord of clay in half lengthwise; you will get an interesting play of lines that you can then apply in a spiral on a ball. These beads can be smoothed if you wish. E

Type 4

Cut cross-sections of the square cord and apply them side by side to a ball of clay. By playing with concentric circles and spirals (see page 25), you can create different beads in a range of assorted shades. F

Type 5

Mix concentric circles and lines to create beads in a new style. G

Type 6

Cut slices a bit larger and you will get assorted cubic beads. To vary the size of the beads, you can use different tips on the clay gun and cut longer or shorter slices. H

Vary the colors, remembering that gray plus burgundy equals pink, and green plus gray equals light green.

Finishing the beads

Make holes in the beads before baking. Sand the large round beads without polishing them.

Assembling the necklace

Simply string different beads on the wire, placing the round ones about every 3 inches. At the end, attach the two wires together, crossing them in the crimp beads.

 ADVICE

String the beads without cutting the wire from the spool; this will keep the beads from sliding off. You can cut the wire once the assembly is finished.

Assembling the charm

Attach the beads to the metal ring by knotting the ribbons.

 ADVICE

To make it easier to thread the ribbons through the beads, make sure the hole is big enough and use a scrap of wire folded in half to serve as a needle threader.

A seaside look

Similar to a mosaic, the effect obtained with this technique helps you create lovely pebblelike beads.

Materials for the beads

- One block of pearly white clay
- One block of beige clay
- Quarter block of gold clay
- Quarter block of black clay
- Quarter block of white clay
- Stamp
- Oval cookie cutter, 1 inch long
- Eye-shaped cookie cutter, 2 inches long
- Wooden toothpicks

Materials for assembly

The necklace
- 20-gauge brass wire, 20 inches
- One gold bar-and-ring clasp and two rings
- Six 8mm almond-colored pearly beads
- Four 10mm topaz glass beads
- Twenty-four 4mm ivory-colored bohemian faceted beads
- Pearly 2.5mm seed bead

The bracelet
- Two strands of elastic thread, 0.8mm thick, 8 inches each
- Sixteen 10mm topaz glass beads
- Thirty-two 4mm ivory seed beads

The earrings
- Gold earring components
- Two open twisted rings, 0.8mm diameter

Making the beads

The watercolor mosaic

This technique, also called WACOMO or WCM, was invented by Maggie Maggio. The version presented here is a slightly simpler variation.

1 Make a $1/8$-inch thick clay sheet shaded from white to beige. Place this on top of a white sheet the same size and thickness; place these both on a black sheet the same size and thickness. Run the stack through the clay machine. A

2 Stretch out the resulting sheet to a thickness of $1/8$ inch then to $1/16$ inch. Tear it into little pieces and place them randomly on a sheet of beige clay $1/8$ inch thick.

3 Smooth the whole thing with a roller and set it aside.

The mica shift

1 Prepare the pearly clay using the mica shift technique (see page 23 for instructions), using your chosen motif. You'll want a sheet of clay that's $1/16$ inch thick.

The beads

1 Place a sheet of gold clay $1/16$ thick on your baking support and cut out the leaves, using the pattern given here. B

2 On a piece of cellophane, position the sheet of watercolor mosaic with the single color sheet on top. With the oval cookie cutter, cut out part of the clay, centering the hole,

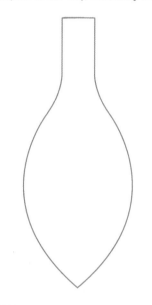

and fill the space you created with an oval of the mica shift clay, with the decorated side face-down. C

3 Attach two pearly ovals to two smaller pieces of gold clay, also oval, with a "tail" at one end, and cut to the same size as the pearly piece.

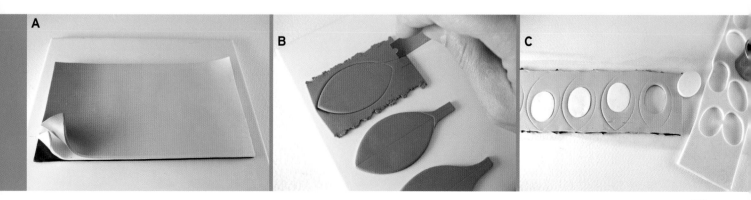

A

B

C

4 Once all the parts are assembled, cut the shapes with a cookie cutter and use the cellophane to position them correctly on the gold base leaves. D

5 Wrap the gold end around a toothpick and texture the wrap with a pen cap or the point of a needle, as desired.

6 Bake the beads according to the manufacturer's instructions.

Finishing the beads

If the crack between the pearly cabochon and its surrounding is too prominent, fill it with a bit of pearly acrylic paint and wipe away the excess with a paper towel.

Sand your pieces well, using up to 2000-grit paper.

Assembling the necklace

Make a loop in the brass wire to attach the clasp with its ring then simply string on the beads following the pattern. E

Assembling the bracelet

1 Make eight polymer beads using the centers you cut from the necklace beads and the remainder of the watercolor mosaic sheet.

2 Attach the watercolor mosaic cabochons to gold base leaves $1/16$ inch thick (cut out following the pattern given here). Wrap each end around a toothpick and give the beads a gentle curved shape by baking them while they are stuck to a glass jar. F

3 String the beads on the elastic thread (as shown in G) then proceed in the same way for the other side. Knot the threads well and hide the knot in a polymer bead.

Assembling the earrings

Make the polymer clay beads like the two small beads for the necklace. Assemble the earrings by simply linking the pendant to the earring component with the jump ring.

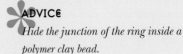
Hide the junction of the ring inside a polymer clay bead.

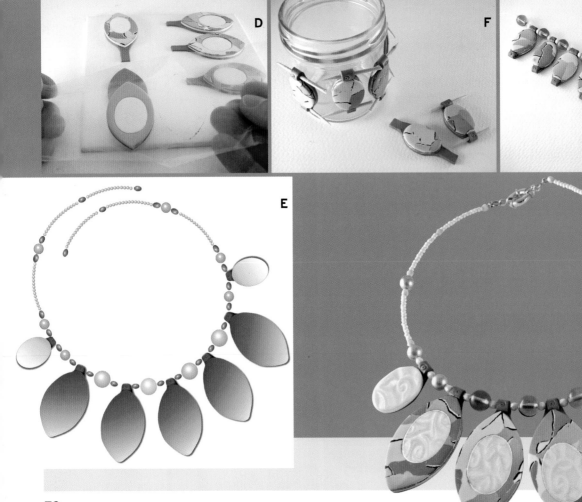

A vivid look

A richly ornamented and brightly colored necklace in fluorescent colors, made with the Hidden Magic technique.

Materials for the beads

The necklace

- One sheet of clay prepared with the Hidden Magic technique (described on page 23)
- Half a block of scrap clay
- One square cookie cutter, 1½ inches on each side
- One square cookie cutter, 1¼ inches on each side
- One square cookie cutter, ¾ inch on each side

Materials for assembly

The necklace

- Beading wire, 28 inches
- 240 green 4mm bohemian faceted beads
- Two black 8mm bohemian faceted beads
- One green 12mm bohemian faceted bead
- One box of seed beads
- Six 4mm metallic round beads
- Two large metal bead caps for 14mm beads
- Two small (4mm) metal bead caps
- Two crimp beads
- 20-gauge brass wire
- One eyepin, ½ inch long
- Round pliers
- Drill, ³⁄₆₄-inch bit

Making the beads

The pillow beads: one large, two small

1 Roll out a scrap base ⅛ inch thick, fold it in half lengthwise, and cut two squares, 1½ inches on each side. Cut off a strip about ¼ inch wide on the right and the bottom of each one of the two squares, then pinch the edges with your thumb and index finger.

2 Put the two sheets of scrap one on top of the other and pinch the border again. A

3 From the smoothed-out Hidden Magic sheet, cut two large squares, 1½ inch on each side, using the cookie cutter. Be sure to select the most interesting areas of clay.

4 Place the scrap tile between the two Hidden Magic tiles, patterns on the outside, and gently pinch the edges together. B

5 You can use a needle to push down the scrap clay if necessary (C). Join the patterned edges together and smooth the joint with your fingertip, a clay shaper, or a small wooden stick.

6 You want the bead to have a nice even pillow shape.

7 With a long needle, pierce the large bead horizontally all the way through. D

✳ ADVICE

To correctly pierce your bead, hold it firmly without squeezing it. Make a hole about halfway through on one side then switch to the other side so that the two holes meet in the middle. Turn the needle gently as you pierce the clay and keep it as straight as possible.

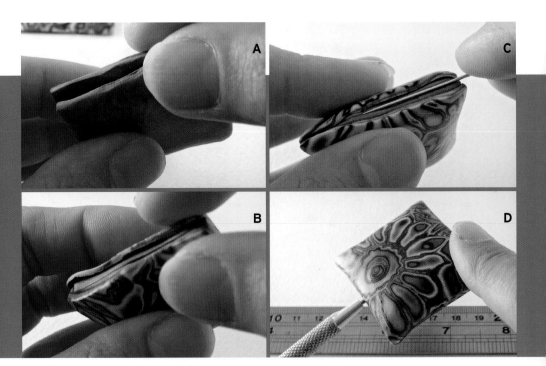

8 Make a hole about ¹/₂ inch deep in the middle of the top of the bead. D

9 Now make two smaller pillow beads using the same method described on page 74.

10 Make a diagonal hole through one little bead, going corner to corner. Make a hole through the other small bead, going side to side. (These smaller beads can be pierced after baking if you prefer.)

The round beads

1 With the leftover Hidden Magic clay, cover one 14mm round bead.

2 Make a hole in it before baking.

3 Bake the piece according to the manufacturer's directions.

4 Lightly sand it without marring the surface then apply a varnish.

The earring beads

1 Make two little pillow beads like the ones for the necklace—but don't make holes in them before baking. Bake the pieces following the manufacturer's directions.

2 Lightly sand them and apply a varnish.

3 With a drill, make a hole through the corner of the pillow, taking care not to go too close to the edge so you don't damage the bead.

Finishing the beads

1 Make a large loop in the brass wire using a pair of round pliers.

2 Put the wire through a large pillow bead, cut the wire about ¹/₂ inch from the edge of the bead, and make another loop on that side. Make sure the green faceted beads can easily pass through these loops before beginning the beading work. E

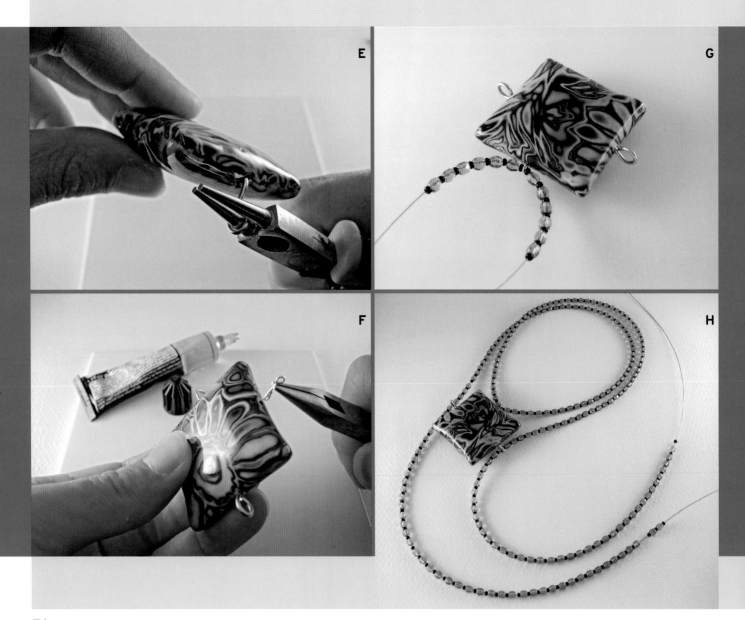

3 On a small 2-inch length of wire you'll fashion the upper attachment: Make a small loop with your pliers. About ¹/₂ inch from this, fold ¹/₂ inch of wire toward the top. Cut off the excess. Attach the loop with a drop of glue after checking that it is in the right position. F

*✲**VARIATION***

The round bead can be a color that matches the pillows, smooth or textured with salt, or covered with mokume gane. You could also replace it with a glass bead.

Assembling the necklace

1 Begin by passing the beading wire through the little ring on the top of the large pillow and putting one seed bead on each side. G

2 Alternate faceted beads and seed beads until you reach the desired length. For the necklace to slip easily over your head, you'll need at least 100 faceted beads on each strand. Adjust the length by adding beads as desired.

3 When you are finished, pass the strands through the opposite metal loops fixed on both sides of the large pillow bead. H

4 Thread onto one strand one small 4mm round bead, one 8mm faceted bead, one bead cup, a large found bead, a bead cup, the small pillow with the hole through the middle, and a small 4mm round bead. Finish with a crimp bead. Trim the excess wire.

5 Assemble the other strand the same way but with a large round polymer bead and the small diagonally pierced pillow bead. I

I

VARIATION

Make a light-colored variation with an opaque and translucent mokume gane and several slices of cane flower.

A mysterious look

Create intriguing images with opalescent clays to give your beads a mysterious look.

Materials for the beads

- One block of pearly white clay
- One block of gold clay
- On block of bronze clay
- Various stamps
- Sharp, flexible knife blade

Materials for assembly

- Eight 4mm Golden Shadow crystal bicones
- Eight 4mm round almond-colored pearly beads
- Eight 3mm round metal beads
- One 8mm almond-colored bead
- One clasp
- One metal tassel
- Ten 14mm metal bead caps
- Five eyepins, 2¾ inches long
- Fourteen 7mm rings
- One large unbroken ring in worked metal, about ¾ inch diameter
- Chain, 12 inches

Making the beads

1 With your three colors of clay, make a circular shaded cane, with the light color in the center (see page 16). A

2 Flatten it with the clay roller to create a sheet about ⅛ inch thick.

3 Imprint the surface with various stamps.

4 Shave off the raised portions and save them to make the round beads. B

5 Fold the sheet in half, with the pattern to the outside, then smooth it with a roller. C

6 Place the sheet onto a baking surface and cut out three large rectangles (1¾ by 1 inch) and two smaller ones (1 by ¾ inch).

7 Use the leftovers from this sheet to make four equal-sized balls and a fifth that's slightly flattened.

8 Cover the balls with the rest of the shaved-off portions and smooth them by rolling them gently in your hands. Poke holes in them and stick them on pins into a ball of aluminum foil to bake them without marring them.

9 Bake according to the manufacturer's instructions.

Finishing the beads

The ghostly effect emerges more fully after careful finishing. Sand the beads with up to 2000-grit paper. Apply several coats of varnish—even if you don't want to sand the beads, it's recommended that you varnish them.

Assembling the necklace

Mount the round beads on the eyepins and add, both above and below, a crystal bicone, round 4mm pearl, round 3mm metal bead, and a bead cap. Close the pin with a second loop.

Attach the rings to the rectangular sheets, taking care to make holes a little larger than the thickness of the rings. Do this carefully so you don't break the clay rectangles.

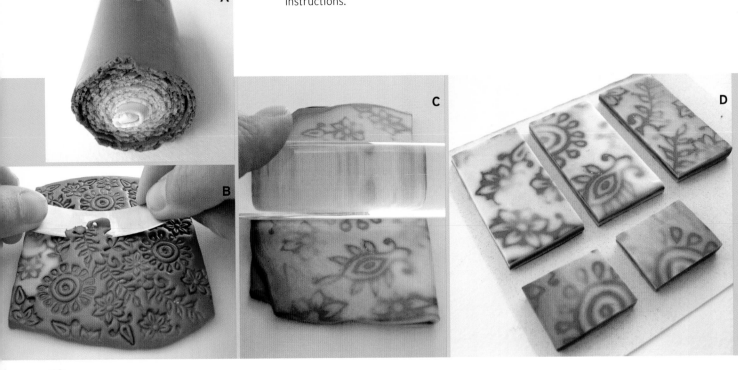

An earthy look

Bones, leather, and wood—natural materials to create an earthy look.

Materials for the beads

- One block of beige clay
- One block of translucent clay
- One block of chocolate-brown clay
- Half a block of gold clay
- Various stamps
- Black and burnt sienna acrylic paint
- Round cookie cutters of different diameters
- Varnish

Materials for assembly

The necklace

- Black or dark brown waxed cotton cord, 8 feet
- One 10mm diameter round bead in a matching color for the clasp

The bracelet (see page 83)

- Black or dark brown waxed cotton cord, 6½ feet

The charm

- Scraps of black or dark brown waxed cotton cord
- Matching ribbon, 10 inches
- One large bronze clasp

Making the imitation bone

1 Stack a sheet of white clay and a sheet of translucent clay and make a sheet ⅛ inch thick.

2 Cut it in half, stack the halves again, and put it through the clay machine set at ⅛ inch. A

3 Continue doing this until you have fine but still visible lines along the edges. B

4 Cut fine slices from the side of this block and place them side by side, flat sides down, on a sheet of marbled beige and translucent clay that's ⅛ inch thick. Smooth it and cut out the beads in the desired shape. C

5 Texture the surface by making lines with a needle, marking the clay with abstract designs or figured stamps, as shown. Bake according to the manufacturer's instructions. D

6 Once the beads have cooled, patina the crevices with black acrylic paint mixed with burnt sienna and quickly wipe off the excess with a paper towel. E

7 Sand the beads and polish the surfaces.

Making the imitation leather

1 Leather is relatively easy to imitate. In a chocolate-brown clay sheet ⅛ inch thick, make decorative prints with stamps then texture the empty spaces by pressing a crumpled paper towel into the clay. F

2 Cut out the beads the size you want them and bake according to the manufacturer's instructions.

3 Once the beads have cooled, patina them the same way you did the imitation bone beads.

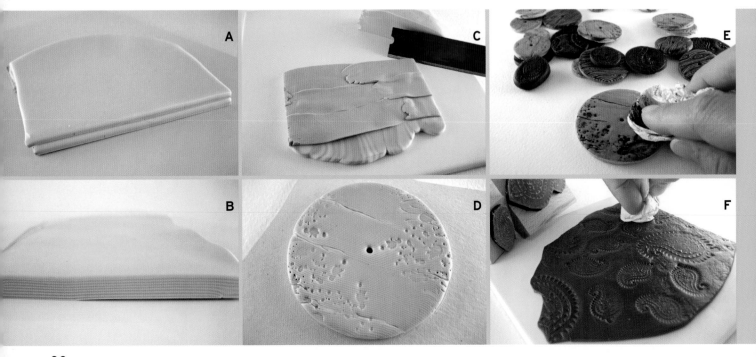

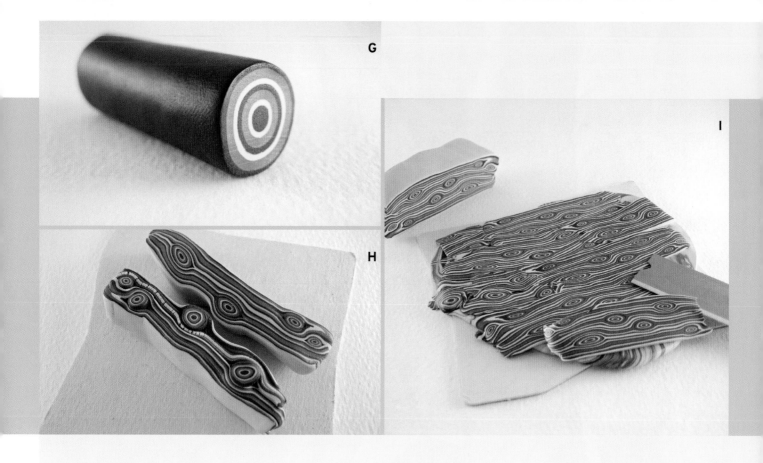

Making the imitation wood

To make the imitation wood, use three colors: chocolate-brown, beige, and gold.

1 Make a cane with a target pattern with sheets of the three colors then reduce it. The slices you cut off this cane will form the knots in the wood. B

2 Create a clay sheet ⅛ inch thick by stacking the three colors. Cut several bands of identical size out of this sheet.

3 Set these bands side by side, with like colors facing each other, inserting the cane "knots" between them—make sure that the knots are next to two sheets of the same color. H

4 Use the "wood" block of clay as you did the "bone" block, cutting out sheets to apply to a base. I

5 Texture the beads with the point of a needle, making "grain" lines the same direction as the color streaks.

6 After baking, finish the beads as you did the other two imitations.

Making the beads

1 Make one sheet of bone, one of leather, and one of wood.

2 Smooth them all with a clay roller and cut out the beads with a cookie cutter.

The necklace

- Bone: one 2-inch circle, two 1½-inch circles, and two 1-inch circles
- Leather: two 2-inch circles and two 1½-inch circles
- Wood: Two 2-inch circles and two 1½-inch circles

The charm

- Bone: Two large oval beads
- Leather: One charm
- Wood: One round bead

ADVICE

Pierce the beads in the center before applying the patina.

3 Texture the surface by making lines with the needle and marking the clay with abstract or figured stamps. Bake according to the manufacturer's instructions. J

4 Once the beads have cooled, apply a patina to the crevices with black acrylic paint mixed with burnt sienna and quickly wipe off the excess with a paper towel.

5 Sand lightly. If the acrylic patina on the false leather was well wiped away, it is not necessary to sand it. Sand the other two materials to reveal their subtle color variations.

6 Apply a coat of varnish to protect the patina—working only in the crevices to avoid a plastic look. These materials are much prettier with a satiny—not a shiny—finish.

J

L

K

M

Assembling the necklace

1 In the middle of the cotton cord, make a loop, checking that the round bead will pass through it, and knot the two strands together.

2 Knot the two strands without a bead at 2 inches, then 2 inches farther.

3 Cross the two strands through the smallest bone bead. K

4 Continue with the small false wood bead, placing it on the top, then tighten the two cords. Continue in this way, being careful to put the large central bead on the top.

5 Make your necklace symmetrical and finish with the round bead for the clasp.

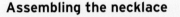

❋ ADVICE

Apply a bit of varnish to the ends of the cut cord to keep them from unraveling.

Assembling the bracelet

1 Begin with a loop and proceed as with the necklace, but in an asymmetrical fashion; mix light and dark and small and large, placing the small ones on the top.

2 Finish the bracelet with a round bead, as for the necklace. M

Assembling the charm

Attach the beads directly to the clasp with ribbon or cotton cord. Avoid rings and other metal pins that cannot handle rubbing. Add ribbons, applying a touch of varnish to the cut ends.

A free-spirited look

Create beautiful imitations of semiprecious stones, such as the turquoise in this long necklace.

Materials for the beads

The imitation turquoise

- One block of turquoise clay
- A bit of emerald-green clay
- A bit of white clay
- Gold metallic foil
- Black and burnt sienna acrylic paint

The textured and patina beads

- Two identical textured sheets
- One block of black clay
- Bright aqua-green acrylic paint
- Gold acrylic paint
- Varnish
- Sponge
- Drill, fitted with polishing felt

Materials for assembly

The necklace

- Eight 6mm round almond-colored pearly beads
- Three 8mm round almond-colored pearly beads
- Thirteen eyepins, 2¼ inches long
- Seven headpins, 1½ inches long
- Thirteen clasps
- Eighteen rings, 1½ inch diameter
- Eight varied charms
- Twenty 4mm tourmaline bicones
- Thirty 3mm round metal beads
- Six 8mm metal bead caps
- Large chain, 20 inches
- Five 7mm jump rings
- Imitation turquoise suede, 20 inches

Making the beads

The imitation turquoise

1 Work your clay until it is very soft. Make a fine marbled mixture of the three colors then create squiggly shavings of the clay by rolling the end of a sausage-shaped lump between your thumb and index finger. A

2 Add bits of gold foil and mix with the tips of your fingers, being careful not to crush the bits of clay.

3 Add a bit of black and burnt sienna paint; the two colors should not be mixed. Gently "stir" the paint into the clay without crushing the clay. B

4 From the mixture, form five large oval beads, about 1 inch in diameter, and three small ones, ½ to ¾ inch thick. Don't smooth the surfaces of the beads too much; you want the beads to have an unfinished look.

5 Bake according to the manufacturer's directions then make holes in the beads.

6 Let the beads soak for thirty minutes in lukewarm water. Then scrub the surfaces with a sponge. Let the beads dry, then sand them with a miniature drill fitted with polishing felt. For a smoother look, finish with 1000-grit sandpaper. Don't apply more than one coat of varnish so the beads aren't too shiny. C

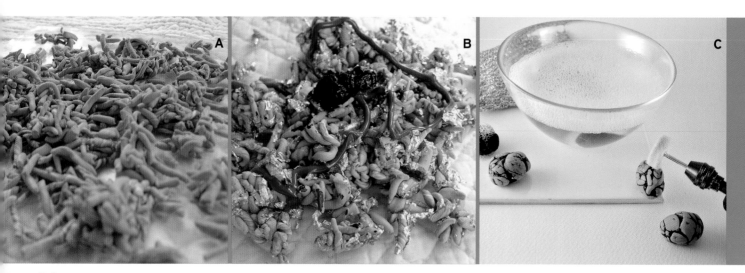

The textured and patina beads

1 From the black clay, make four cylinders of equal size. D

2 Roll them across a textured sheet, preferably wet or brushed with talcum powder, pushing with the second textured sheet in a firm, continuous motion so that the pattern is firmly imprinted on the bead. E

3 Put the beads in the freezer for five or so minutes before making holes in them to avoid smudging the pattern. You can also make the holes after baking if you wish. In this case, bake the beads set in a piece of paper that's folded like an accordion to keep from marring the patterns. F

4 After baking, apply a patina to the beads with acrylic paint (see page 19 for instructions).

5 Make two flat round beads the same way, each 1/2 inch wide, by pressing a ball of clay between the two textured sheets.

Assembling the necklace

1 Mount the oval turquoise beads and textured beads on the large eyepins, adding small beads on both sides. G and H

2 Add a piece of chain four links long on each side of the turquoise beads.

3 Continue the pattern, alternating turquoise beads and textured beads.

4 Assemble three tassel charms using an eyepin, two 3-inch lengths of suede folded in half, a cylindrical bead cap, and several beads. Finish the attachment with a loop and small clasp. Add a metal charm and attach these drop charms to the chain, spacing them out. I

5 Mount the other charms on the clasps and attach them to the large chain links. J

The bracelet

Materials

- Four large (½-inch diameter) round imitation turquoise polymer beads
- Four textured polymer cylinders, ½ inch in diameter and about ¾ inch long
- Four 6mm round beads with loops to hold charms
- Four charms
- Four headpins, 1½ inches long
- Four 4mm rings
- Four 4mm tourmaline bicones
- Eight 3mm round metal beads
- Seed beads
- Sixteen 8mm bead caps
- Clear elastic thread, 0.8mm thick, 8 inches
- Jewelry glue

1 Thread the seed beads and small beads onto the headpins and finish with a loop attached to a ring. Add a metal charm and attach the whole thing to a charm-holding bead.

2 The assembly is done simply by alternating turquoise beads and textured beads, with bead caps on both sides of each. Between each pair of polymer beads, put either a charm-holder bead or a round bead.

3 Finish by knotting the elastic; use a needle to help you adjust it well. Fix it with a drop of jewelry glue and trim the ends. Hide the knot in the hole of a large bead.

The earrings

Materials

- Two flat textured polymer beads
- Two ear wires
- Six 3mm round metal beads
- Two headpins, 2 inches long
- Two 4mm tourmaline bicones
- Four bronze seed beads

Mount the beads on the headpins following the pattern and attach them to the ear wires. K

The charm

Materials

- One 10mm round and one 1-inch-long oval imitation turquoise bead
- One textured polymer cylinder, ½ inch long
- One flat textured polymer bead
- Thin satin ribbon, ochre and brown, 8 inches
- Thin ochre organza ribbon, 8 inches
- Brown waxed cotton cord, 8 inches
- Turquoise waxed cotton cord, 8 inches
- One 6mm round metal bead
- One headpin, 1½ inches long
- One eyepin, 2¾ inches long
- Two 7mm rings
- Four 4mm tourmaline bicones
- Five 3mm round metal beads
- Two 8mm bead caps
- Several bronze seed beads
- One large clasp, 1¼ inches long

1 Knot the ribbons and the cord directly onto the clasp attachment; attach the other charms with 7mm rings.

2 Assemble the charms following the pattern. L

ADVICE

To keep the ribbons and cords from fraying, apply a bit of varnish to the ends. Sparkly fingernail polish can also produce a nice effect.

Working with
Canes

A pure look

Create tiles featuring subtle layers of flower patterns and use them to make rings and pins—or this beautiful choker.

Materials for the beads

- Flower canes, one style or a variety of styles
- Block of translucent clay
- Square cookie cutter, 1/2 inch on each side

Materials for assembly

- Memory wire, 14 inches
- Fifteen 6mm rings
- Two 7mm rings
- Fourteen large amethyst seed beads
- 20-gauge wire, 6 inches
- Round pliers
- Drill, 3/64-inch bit

Making the beads

1 With the translucent clay, make a sheet 1/8 inch thick. Choose your canes; here we are using an assortment of flowers in pink, plum, and khaki green.

2 Lay canes slices on the sheet, creating any design you wish—it should be full, but you don't have to cover every gap and space. A

3 Place another sheet of translucent clay 1/16 inch thick on top of the first sheet, being careful not to create air bubbles. B

4 Lay out slices of a different pattern, or the same pattern, on the sheet, this time leaving plenty of space between them. C

5 Place a sheet of cellophane or parchment paper on the surface of the clay and press gently with your fingers to even out any bumps. Smooth it carefully to get as even a sheet as possible. You can use a roller to completely eliminate any bumps, or the sheet could be put through a clay machine.

If you use a machine, set it at the depth of the sheet and put the clay through in one direction. Then turn it a quarter turn and run it through again, one notch thinner. The sheet you'll get will be very smooth, but also very thin—you'll need to lay it over another smooth sheet of translucent clay to create more solid pieces. You can use this type of sheet for many projects.

6 Cut nine squares of identical size with the cookie cutter (or a knife) while the clay is on the baking surface. D

7 Bake according to the manufacturer's instructions.

8 Sand very carefully and apply a coat of varnish to the tiles, then make holes in them as shown in the photo on page 91.

Assembling the necklace

1 Fasten the tiles to each other using 6mm rings.

2 Make a spiral at the end of the 20-gauge wire, string on the 4mm beads, and finish with an identical spiral on the other end. Attach this to the clay tiles with three 6mm rings.

3 Attach this piece directly to the memory wire using two 7mm rings.

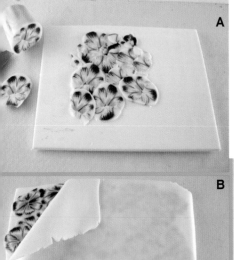

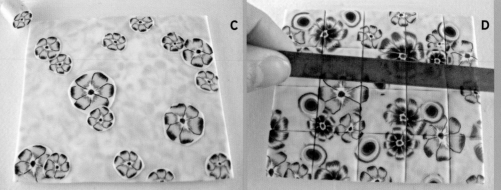

A B C D

A romantic look

Give a rounded shape to patterned sheets of clay to make button-style beads, great for creating rings and earrings.

Materials for the beads

- One block of translucent mokume gane (see page 22)
- One flower cane made with a clay gun (see page 25)
- One block of gold clay
- Leftover clay
- Round cookie cutters, 1¾ inches and 1¼ inches in diameter
- Five mounting eyepins
- Four different-sized lightbulbs
- Varnish
- Cellophane
- Liquid Fimo clay
- Small paintbrush
- Knife
- Round pliers

Materials for assembly

- Chain, 8 inches
- Eight 7mm rings
- Three 4mm rings (for the charm)
- Clasp

Making the beads

First baking

1 Prepare the sheet, creating a marble of left-over clay in the same shades as the cane and covering it with tinted translucent mokume gane. Lay some slices of flower cane on the mokume gane. A

> ✿ **ADVICE**
> *Avoid using a color with too strong a contrast or a brownish color for the underlay, since this may show through the mokume gane after baking.*

2 Put a sheet of cellophane on the clay and smooth it with your finger before finishing with a roller. B

3 Cut four small circles and one large circle from the sheet using the cookie cutters.

4 Put the circles on a rounded surface—lightbulbs work particularly well for this, but any similar glass surface will do. Bake according to the manufacturer's instructions. C

5 Make a small clay flower for the clasp, which can be attached with three 4mm rings.

Second baking

1 From a sheet of gold clay 1/16 inch thick, cut four small circles and one large one using cookie cutters. Place a metal eyepin on the upper part of each disc and cover it with a bit of clay to support the curved clay disks. Dab a bit of liquid polymer clay on the edges of the disks then set them in place. D

2 Clean up the cut edges with a knife and close any gaps by smoothing with the flat of a knife blade.

3 Bake according to the manufacturer's instructions.

Finishing the assembly

1 Take out the pins to sand and polish the beads, then re-insert them. E

2 Close up the other end of the pins with a loop and link the different attachments together with rings. F

3 Add a length of chain with a clasp.

An autumn look

A richly patterned look . . . made by combining flower, leaf, and branching spiral canes.

Materials for the necklace

- One block of copper clay
- Leftover green clay
- One brown flower cane (see page 26)
- Two leaf canes (see page 27)
- One spiral cane (see page 26)
- Round cookie cutter, 2 inches in diameter (for the medallion)
- Round cookie cutter, ¾ inch in diameter (for the rounded side beads)
- Cellophane

Materials for assembly

The necklace

- Twelve 6mm dark green pearly beads
- Four 8mm gold-colored pearly beads
- Sixteen 4mm beige crystal bicones
- Eight 4mm large gold seed beads
- Four 2mm gold seed beads
- Copper chain, 9 inches
- Two large, decorated, unbroken rings, ¾ inch diameter
- Clasp
- Twenty 7mm jump rings
- Four eyepins, 2¾ inches
- Four eyepins, 1½ inches
- Drill, ⁵⁄₆₄-inch bit

The central medallion

1 Make a marbled base with your green left-over clay, in a thick sheet.

2 Cut a large circle with the cookie cutter.

3 Place the underlying elements—here a series of slices of spiral cane—on the right side of the circle. A

4 Place slices of the leaf cane on the left.

5 Place flower cane slices in the middle, arranging them any way you wish. When the slices are all placed, lay a piece of cellophane over the whole thing and smooth out the most obvious bumps with your finger. Finish by going over it gently with a roller until the gaps between the patterned slices disappear. B

6 Texture the medallion with the point of a needle if you wish. Tiny dots were made here. C

7 Bake according to the manufacturer's instructions.

✱ ADVICE

To make translucent clay as invisible as possible on a colored background, cut as thin a slice as you can from the cane. You can also place the slice between two sheets of cellophane, pressing to make it thinner, then cutting out the translucent parts with a knife. To avoid tearing the piece, set it in place while it's still attached to the cellophane. After pressing the slice with your finger, very carefully pull away the cellophane.

The rounded side beads

1 Cut out two circles with the cookie cutter from a sheet of copper clay ¹⁄₈ inch thick.

2 From a simple leaf cane, cut seven very thin slices and place them in a circle, the tips just barely extending past the edge of the copper circle. D

3 From a six-petal flower cane, cut one slice, and use a needle to texture the transparent triangles that separate the petals or a knife to remove them. Place the flower in the center of the leaves and texture it with the point of a needle.

4 Place the beads on a gently rounded support, such as a lightbulb (see page 92) and bake according to the manufacturer's instructions. Sand the beads, polish them, or apply a coat of varnish. Make holes in them, following the pattern. E

Assembling the necklace

1 On the two longer eyepins, string the beads according to the pattern (E).

2 On the two smaller eyepins, string the beads in the same way and close the pin with a loop.

3 With a drill, make four holes in the medallion, two on each side, near the top, as shown. E

4 Insert four 7mm jump rings, then add a 4mm seed bead and the long eyepins. Close up the rings.

5 Proceed in the same way to attach the two small polymer beads. The two rings at the top are without seed beads and are linked to the smaller eyepins.

6 Add the large decorated rings, attaching them to the eyepins with two 7mm jump rings.

7 Finish the rest of the way around the necklace with the two pieces of chain in the desired length, attaching them with two 7mm jump rings.

D

E

The bracelet

Materials

- Four small flowered disks, identical to those in the necklace
- Six 6mm dark green pearly beads
- Twelve 4mm gold-colored crystal bicones
- Fourteen large (4mm) gold seed beads
- One copper clasp
- Sixteen 7mm jump rings
- Six copper eyepins, 1 inch

1 Make holes in the beads following the pattern. F

2 String the beads on the six eyepins, following the pattern, and close with a loop. F

3 Attach the pins to the beads with 7mm jump rings. Put a large seed bead on each ring.

4 Finish the bracelet with one ring on each side and attach the clasp with another ring.

✳ ADVICE

To avoid breaking the polymer clay bead when you put a ring in it, make sure the hole is larger than the ring you're using and pass it through the front hole of the bead. This way the edge of the hole that could chip will be on the back of the bead; the defect won't be visible.

The ring

Materials

- One round cookie cutter, 1 ¼ inches
- One ring base with a flat top
- Slices of leaf and flower canes
- Bit of copper clay
- Liquid polymer clay
- One small lightbulb

1 On a small lightbulb, apply a 1¼-inch circle of copper clay.

2 Place ten thin slices of leaf cane around the circle, going over the edges a tiny bit, and place the flower slice in the center, proceeding as with the rounded beads in the necklace. Press lightly to make the patterns stick without deforming them and texture the flower with a needle.

3 Bake according to the manufacturer's instructions, propping the bulb up in a glass container.

4 Once the clay has cooled, dab the interior with a bit of liquid polymer and add a ball of copper clay in the hollow. Push the flat part of the ring completely into the copper clay and smooth out the possible cracks.

5 Bake according to the manufacturer's instructions, with the ring pointing up.

6 Sand and polish.

A changeable look

Use clay sheets with patterns on both sides to make these reversible millefiori pieces.

Materials for the beads

The necklace (see page 101)

- One block of turquoise clay
- Brown and turquoise flower canes in different sizes (see page 26)
- Metallic powders in three shades of brown or bronze
- Blue metallic powder
- Stamp
- Oval cookie cutter, 1½ inches long

The bracelet (see page 101)

- Same materials as for the necklace
- Fine salt
- Two-part resin

Materials for assembly

All the finishings are bronze-colored.

The necklace

- Chain, 20 inches
- Clasp and two 7mm rings
- Eleven 7mm rings

The bracelet

- Twenty-three headpins, 1½ inches
- Fourteen 4mm golden topaz crystal bicones
- Four 4mm blue zircon crystal bicones
- Ten 9-by-8mm bronze pearly nuggets
- Forty-six 3mm round metal beads
- Sixteen 6mm bead caps
- Twenty-four 4mm rings
- Seven 7mm rings

The earrings

- Two ear wires
- Two 4mm rings
- Two 7mm rings
- Two 3mm turquoise seed beads
- Two polymer oval reversible beads

The ring

- Thin brown aluminum wire, 8 inches
- 26-gauge brass wire, 8 inches
- Glue
- Drill, ⁵⁄₆₄-inch bit
- Brown and turquoise acrylic paint pens

Making the beads

The patterned sheet

1 On a marbled background, lay out several slices of one of the patterned canes. Large brown flowers with the translucent parts removed were used here.

2 Do the same with the contrasting flower cane—turquoise flowers were used here—placing them in the empty spaces. A

3 Use medium-sized flower slices to fill in any gaps, then small ones to do the same. (For the small flowers, it isn't necessary to cut out the translucent clay between the petals, especially if your slices are very thin.) Don't hesitate to overlap the different patterns slightly to create a sense of depth.

4 Smooth the sheet to eliminate the gaps between the slices—first with your index finger on cellophane, then very lightly with a clay roller.

5 Place the sheet directly on the baking surface, patterned side down. B

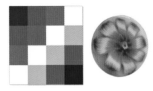

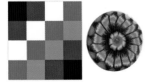

 ADVICE

To make sure no air bubbles form between the sheet and the baking surface, place a piece of glass on top and push all the bubbles to the edges with the roller. If you notice that air has stayed trapped, lightly peel off the clay and start again. Remember, an air bubble will create a hollow space in the baked piece.

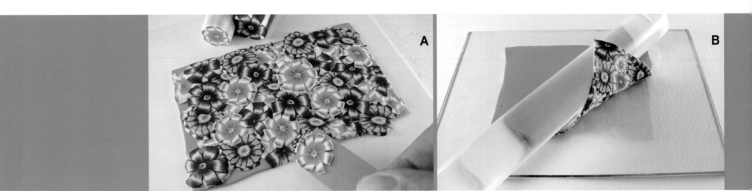

A

B

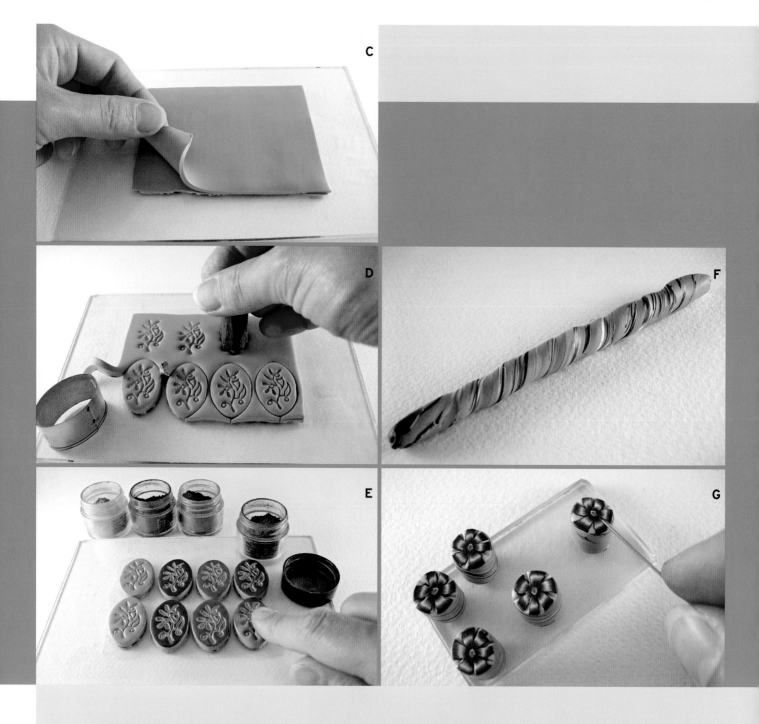

C

D

F

E

G

6 Lay a sheet of turquoise clay that's ⅛ inch thick on the back of the patterned sheet. C

7 Imprint this sheet using a stamp brushed with blue metallic powder. D

8 Cut out ovals with the cookie cutter and apply to six of them contrasting metallic powder to the backgrounds. Use the tip of your finger, taking care not to get powder in the crevices of the pattern. Then do the same with five more ovals, using the blue powder. For the necklace, you'll need six beads with a brown background and five with a blue background. E

9 Bake according to the manufacturer's instructions.

The beads for the charm bracelet
1 With the leftover clay, make a marbled snake shape and cut from it equal-sized sections. F

2 On each face of the sections, apply a thin slice of flower cane. Texture the petals with the point of a needle. G

3 Cut slices of these canes and smooth them with a wet piece of glass to make them very flat and limit the sanding needed later.

4 Bake according to the manufacturer's instructions then color the edges with acrylic paint pens.

Finishing the beads
Sand the sides and the faces and apply a coat of varnish over the powdered parts. You can then apply resin to the faces, or apply two or three coats of Kato Polyclay using a heat gun to set them.

Assembling the necklace
Simply attach the ovals to the chain, alternating beads with a brown background

(powdered side up) and those with a blue background (patterned side up). This will give the piece patterned and metallic beads on both sides—but one side will be predominantly blue and the other predominantly brown.

Assembling the bracelet

Attach the different beads on the headpins as shown (H) and attach them with little rings directly onto the large chain links.

Assembling the ring

1 Make an oval bead ¹/₄ inch thick. Make two holes, ¹/₂ inch apart, in each side.

2 Cut two brown aluminum wires 4 inches long and attach them together by wrapping them with thinner brass wire. Tuck the end of the wire inside of the work. Check the size of the ring before cutting off the ends.

3 Fold the ends of the wire toward the middle at a 90-degree angle about ¹/₂ inch from the end. I

4 Attach the aluminum wires in the holes of the bead with glue. Let them dry.

Assembling the earrings

The beads are identical to those of the necklace. You simply need to make two and attach them to ear wires with a ring, on which you will put a turquoise seed bead.

A fresh look

Use slices of flower cane to create a fresh flower bouquet to wear as a pin or on a necklace.

Materials for the beads

- Several complementary flower canes
- Drill, ³⁄₆₄-inch bit

Materials for assembly

The necklace

- One 10mm round pearly gray bead
- Four 6mm round mauve pearly beads

The bouquet

- Two 6mm round pearly mauve beads
- Seven 4mm round pearly mauve beads
- Seventeen 4mm crystal beads the same colors as the canes
- One box of 4mm seed beads, amethyst mix
- 26-gauge pink brass wire, 5 feet
- 20-gauge pink brass wire, 14 inches
- One magnetic clasp and two rings
- Rubber jewelry cord covered in burgundy velvet, 3mm in diameter, 14 inches

The pin

- Two 6mm round pearly mauve beads
- Two 4mm round pearly mauve beads
- Six 4mm crystal bicones the same colors as the canes
- One box of matching 4mm seed beads
- 26-gauge pink brass wire, 5 feet
- Fibula pin with fretwork top

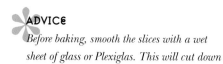

✳ VARIATION

The necklace can be made with small drop beads simply cut out of a sheet with the cap of a pen or marker.

Making the beads

1 From different complementary flower canes, cut thin slices and put them on a piece of cardboard.

2 Cut out the triangle of translucent clay that separates the petals of the largest slices. A

3 Bake according to the manufacturer's instructions.

✳ ADVICE

Before baking, smooth the slices with a wet sheet of glass or Plexiglas. This will cut down considerably on the sanding you'll have to do.

Finishing the beads

1 Sand the beads very lightly; you want to keep the matte appearance.

2 Make two holes in the center of each flower, as though it were a button, using a drill.

Assembling the necklace

1 Use brass wire that can pass through the velvet cord. Make a loop at one end and put a ring on it. String on one large seed bead, then 4 inches of cord, one large seed bead, one bicone, one round 6mm pearly bead, one bicone, and one large seed bead.

2 Continue with ³⁄₄ inch of cord and one large seed bead, one bicone, one round 6mm pearly bead, one bicone, and one large seed bead.

3 Add 6 inches of cord, one seed bead, one 6mm pearl, one seed bead, one 10mm pearl, one seed bead, one 6mm pearl, and one seed bead. B

4 Finish with a cord 4 inches long, one seed bead, one loop, and one ring. Attach the magnetic clasp.

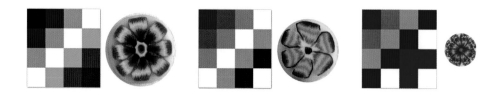

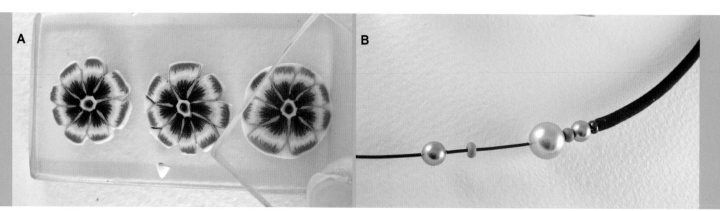

A

B

The necklace bouquet

1 Begin at the center of a length of brass wire folded in half. Thread the wire through the center of a button, add a seed bead, then thread it out through the other hole. Twist the two strands of wire together about $^1/_2$ inch. C

2 Proceed on the two wires, making sure that they are never next to each other without being twisted together (if they are, your work won't be as sturdy).

3 Mix the size and color of the flowers, adding round pearls, colored crystal beads, and seed beads as you wish to create a pleasing arrangement.

4 Once the bouquet is finished, center it on the necklace and wind the two free ends around the cord. Add several beads if you want, and trim the wire. Make sure wire ends aren't exposed to poke you when you're wearing the piece.

5 Attach the other end of the bouquet by twisting two flowers on long stems on opposite sides of the cord together. Do the same in the center for the best hold. Finish your work by spreading out the beads until they look the way you want them to.

Assembling the pin

1 The assembly of the fibula pin is done using the same basic method as the necklace; simply pass the wire through one of the holes in the fretwork top before attaching the next bead. D

2 Begin in the middle, adjusting the length of the wires and the size of the beads to create a nice composition. E

3 Once the bouquet is finished, make a twist 1 inch long and cut the wires. Attach the fretwork top to the pin by rebending the hooks intended for this purpose with a pair of flat pliers.

An incandescent look

Create flat beads, as pretty as pieces of candy, with slices of cane.
The colors are emphasized by the black background.

Materials for the beads

- Clay gun with round tip
- Different colors of clay: black, gray,
  pearly white, red, and burgundy
- Oval cookie cutter, 1 ½ inches by 2 inches
- Round cookie cutter, ¾ inch
- Rounded glass container

Materials for assembly

The necklace (see page 107)

- Eight 8mm red magic or wonder beads
- Eight 8mm gray magic or wonder beads
- Red waxed cotton cord, 6 feet
- Black waxed cotton cord, 6 feet

The bracelet (see page 106)

- Elastic cord, 10 inches
- Drill, ³⁄₃₂-inch bit

✱ ADVICE

To get even concentric circles, place a series of two colors in the clay gun, then proceed as described.

Making the beads for the necklace

1 Place a series of colored sections about ¹⁄₃ inch thick in the clay gun and add the medium-sized round tip. A

2 Cut the cord you get into sections 1 inch long and place these side by side on a sheet of black clay that's ¹⁄₈ inch thick.

3 Roll the sheet up, taking care to not move the cords or create empty spaces inside. Reduce the resulting cane until it's about 1 inch or so in diameter. Cut off a 1-inch-long section then reduce the remainder again until it's about ¹⁄₂ inch in diameter. B

4 From the thicker cane, cut slices ¹⁄₈ inch thick and lay them on a piece of parchment paper. Smooth out their surfaces with a piece of wet glass or Plexiglas. Do the same with the thinner cane. C

5 Make individual sheets of clay in the colors you used for the canes and cut circles out of them with the round cookie-cutter. Smooth these circles with the glass.

6 Bake all the beads according to the maker's instructions.

Making the beads for the bracelet

1 Make a marbled sheet with the scraps of colors used to make the canes. Lay slices like those in the necklace on the sheet, starting with the largest, adding the smaller ones, then filling in the space with little circles cut from one-color cords. D

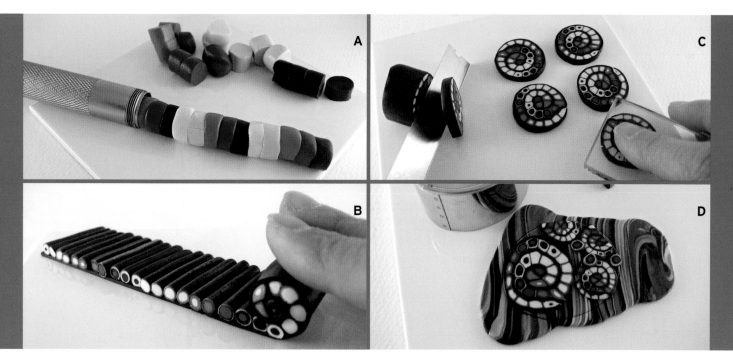

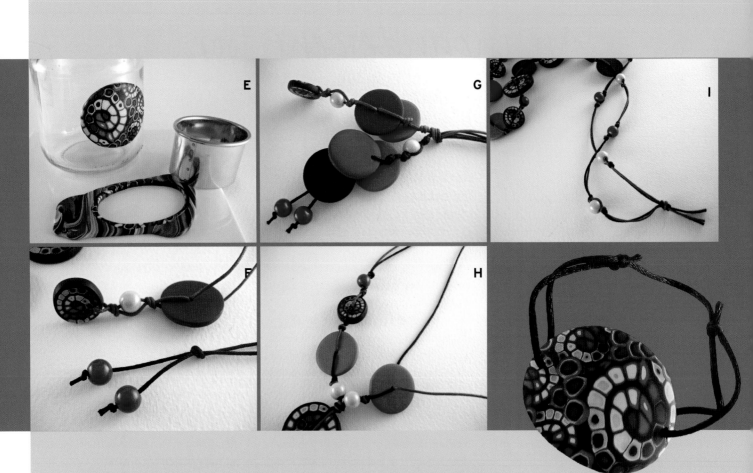

2 Place a sheet of cellophane on the work, press to smooth out any bumps with your fingertips, then smooth it all with the roller until there are no separations between the slices of cane.

3 Cut out a shape with the cookie cutter and apply it to the side of a rounded glass container to bake it. The piece will stick to the glass, but after it has baked and cooled it will come off very easily. E

Finishing the beads

Sand the beads lightly on a firm support, keeping their matte look. Make holes in the one-color beads: five with holes in the center and the others with holes on the edges (to make charms). Make one of the small patterned beads into a charm; pierce all the others in the centers.

Assembling the necklace

1 Fold the red cord in two and attach a polymer charm. Add a magic bead on one strand and knot it again. Add a flat one-color bead and a charm. F

2 Cut the black cord in two and knot one red bead at each end before knotting the two strands together. Attach the charms, separated by knots, and finish by knotting together the two black strands and two red strands. G

3 Attach the flat disks by crossing the strands through the central hole and knotting them tightly against the bead. H

4 Continue, alternating flat one-color beads, patterned beads, and small magic beads.

5 Finish by stringing on and knotting magic beads, spaced out on the lengths. Finish with a knot. I

Assembling the bracelet

1 Make a hole on each side of the bead, at least 1/8 inch from the edge.

2 Thread the cord through and make a sliding knot on each side: With the end of the strand coming out of the bead, make two loops around the strand going into the bead, then pass the end back through the loops, entering on the side closest to the bead. Gently tighten the knot and cut 1/2 inch from the end. To adjust your bracelet, simply slide the knots back and forth.

ADVICE
To pierce the beads exactly in the center, use a circle of paper folded into quarters. Mark the center of the bead with a needle before finishing with a drill large enough to let two cotton cords pass through the hole.

A springtime look

Mold your slices of cane to make realistic petals, like the poppies of this necklace.

Materials for the beads

- One poppy (or other flower) cane
- One block of black clay
- Leftover clay
- Round cookie cutter, the size of the chosen cane
- Needles
- Pliers

Materials for assembly

- Beading wire, 30 inches
- Six red faceted teardrop-shaped beads
- Forty-six 4mm red faceted beads
- One tube of red seed beads
- Eight black seed beads
- Two double rings
- One clasp and two 4mm rings
- One extension chain
- Three crimp beads

Making the beads

First baking

1 Take one poppy cane (see page 27 for instructions) and cut very thin slices. Trim away the triangles between the petals.
2 Make a small ball of clay, poke two needles through it, and cover it with a flower. Work directly on the baking surface. A
3 Mold the petals to give them a gentle curve and texture the flowers with a needle.
4 Bake according to the manufacturer's instructions.

Second baking

1 Without taking out the needles, fill in the cracks on the back of the flower with leftover pieces of clay. Place a circle of black clay on the underside of the flower and work it so it matches the shape of the baked poppy. B
2 Trim and smooth the edges with your finger or a clay shaper.
3 Bake again.

Finishing the beads

1 Sand the beads carefully, retaining their matte appearance.
2 Use a pair of pliers to take out the needles. This is much easier to do if the clay is slightly warm.

Assembling the necklace

Fold the wire in two on one of the rings and hold it with a crimp bead over both wires. The assembly is done after this on the two strands of wire, which go through the faceted beads together until they separate at the first poppy. This gives the necklace more hold and prevents the beads from spinning. For the order of the beads, follow the pattern shown in C.

A moody look

These flowers are molded or applied to round beads so they will dance around your neck.

Materials for the beads
- One block of black clay
- One complex flower cane in three sizes
- Needles

Materials for assembly
- Black beading wire, 4 feet
- 140 4mm black faceted beads
- Two 6mm red faceted beads
- Six 4mm red crystal bicones
- One tube of red 2mm seed beads
- One tube of black 2mm seed beads
- One flared silver bead cap
- Eight crimp beads
- One eyepin, 1 ½ inches
- One 4mm metal bead
- Varnish

ADVICE
Pierce these beads after putting them in the freezer for a while or after baking them.

The flower beads
Make the flowers as you did for the previous project (page 108): one large flower, one medium flower, four small flowers, and four round 12mm beads. A

The round beads
Make a round bead from one-color or marbled clay. Apply thin slices of cane to the desired locations and press lightly with a finger to smooth out the ridges (see page 17). Roll the ball gently between the palms of your hands.

Finishing the beads
Sand and apply three coats of varnish.

Assembling the necklace
1 Fold the wire in half and make a loop with the black seed beads, blocked off at the end by a red crystal bicone. B

Continue with three black faceted beads alternating with red seed beads, and add the large flower, the medium-sized flower, and one of the small flowers, separated by two red seed beads, one black faceted bead, and at least two black seed beads.

2 String on one faceted bead, three seed beads, one faceted bead, and another three seed beads, then make a length of forty-two faceted beads alternating with red seed beads. C

3 Now string on the beads that will block the other end of the wire: one small flower and one round bead, surrounded by two crystal bicones. Continue the work to a length of thirty-eight faceted beads alternating with red seed beads. Now thread both strands through the loop at the other end.

4 Make the tassel with three pieces of beading wire about 5 inches long. Fold them in half, thread them through the hold of a mounting eyepin, and hold the whole thing in place with a round metal bead. E

5 On each of the six strands, place five black seed beads, then nine black faceted beads alternating with red seed beads. Place at the end one flower, one round bead, or one 6mm faceted bead, and hold it on with a crimp bead. Pass the eyepin through the bead cover and close it with a loop.

6 Attach the tassel to the loop that you will form after the last round polymer bead. Close it with two crimp beads. F

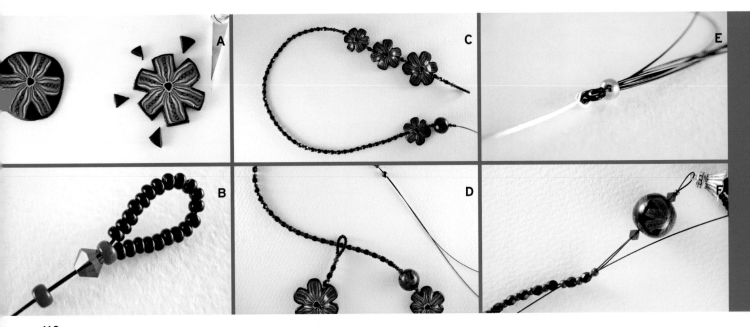

An elegant look

A simple striped cane is shaped and transformed into an elegant flower fibula pin.

Materials

- One block of white clay
- Blocks of Bake and Bend clay in green, white, and beige
- Bit of reddish-brown clay
- Chocolate-brown 26-gauge brass wire, 20 inches
- One fibula pin base, 5 inch
- Golden-rose–colored metallic acrylic paint
- One index card
- Small palette knife
- Flat pliers

✿ ADVICE

So you don't crush the pistil while making the flower, you can prebake it before continuing.

Making the pin

1 Prepare your colors, mixing one-quarter of a block of white polymer clay with three-quarters of a block of Bake and Bend clay (one quarter of each color). This product is very soft clay that is easily marked with fingerprints so it's preferable to work with it while wearing gloves. The advantage to this clay is that after baking, the petals will stay somewhat supple, greatly reducing the risk of breaking.

2 Prepare a striped cane by stacking sheets of green and sheets of white clay. Place one slightly thicker sheet of green clay in the center of the stack. Pinch the ends of the stack and put it in the freezer for a few minutes. A

3 Cut six 2³/₄-inch pins from the brown wire and add little spirals at the tops. Cover this with a little piece of brown clay as shown. B

4 Place some white clay on the head of the fibula pin and shape the head of the pistil as shown. C

5 Cut six petals and etch the center line with an index card folded in half. D

6 Spread out the stamens around the pistil and attach them with a fine brass wire. The stamens can also be made with crystal bicones, held in place with crimp beads. E

7 Put three petals in place and pinch them at the base, then add three more petals in the free spaces.

8 The flower can be molded flat on a baking surface or baked upside-down on a piece of paper. F

Finishing

Patina the petals with a golden-rose-colored acrylic paint. Wipe them off quickly with a paper then gently sand the surfaces.

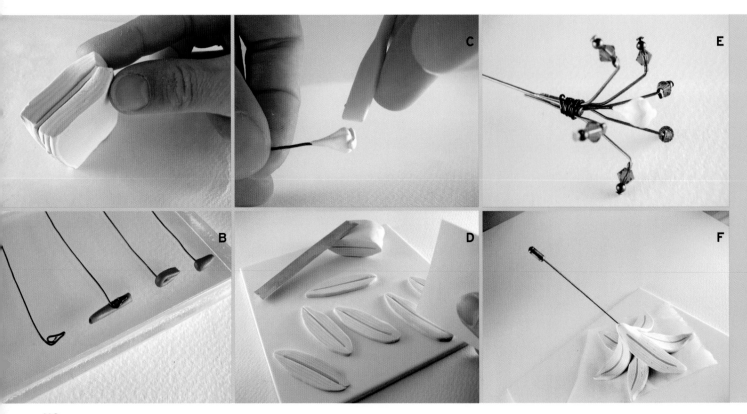

Using a Mix of
Techniques

A bold look

Transfer the design of your choice onto flat beads—it's possible with polymer clay!

Materials for the beads

- One block of white clay
- Half a block of black clay
- Pattern from page 134
- Clay gun with various tips

Materials for assembly

- 20-gauge brass wire, 12 inches
- Two large 4mm seed beads
- One clasp and two 5mm rings
- Hollow buna cord or velvet tube, 8 inches

Making the beads

1 With the clay gun, the circular tip, and the adapter for making hollow beads, make several tubes of black clay and set them in a paper folded like an accordion. A

2 Bake according to the manufacturer's instructions then cut inch-long sections as soon as they come out of the oven, while the clay is still hot and supple. Set these pieces aside.

3 With a laser printer or photocopier, print the pattern from page 134 and cut out the outlines of each bead.

4 Prepare a sheet of white clay ⅛ inch thick and lay a pattern piece of the copies face-down on it. Cut around it, preserving a narrow strip about ¾ inch long at the top part (B). Be careful, depending on the position of the bead in the necklace, the strip of clay has to be oriented differently (refer to the pattern).

5 Place a black cylinder of clay on the strip and roll it in the clay up to the pattern (C).

The white must not be double-thick: If it is, unroll it, cut off the extra piece that's creating the overlap, and roll it up again. Proceed in the same way for all the sheets, keeping them on the baking surface.

6 Place a weight on each pattern (here small pieces of glass are used) and wait at least half an hour before putting them in the oven. For the best transfer, the paper must become a bit oily, letting the pattern show through. D

7 Bake according to the manufacturer's instructions and let the pieces cool down completely before gently removing the papers.

8 Sand the sides and back of each bead.

Assembling the necklace

Simply string the beads onto the wire, placing a large seed bead in between each pair of polymer beads. Cover the rest of the wire with the hollow buna cord.

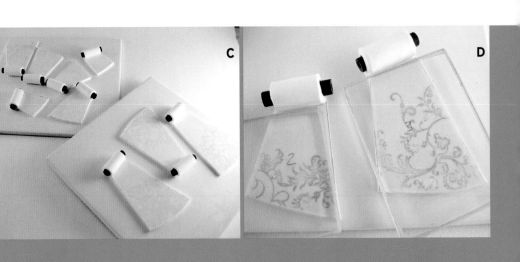

A charmed look

This jewelry combines stamped metal, section beads, and varied colors.

Materials for the beads

- One block of copper clay
- One block of gold clay
- Half a block of burgundy clay
- Half a block of turquoise clay
- "Fatma Hand" pattern (below)
- Clay gun with various tips
- Sparkly copper powder
- Glitter gel pens
- Liquid Fimo clay
- Cellophane
- Resin or varnish

Materials for assembly

The necklace (see page 121)
- Beading wire, four 20-inch strands
- Four-strand clasp
- Eight charms and rings
- Four 4-hole spacer bars
- Sixteen crimp beads
- Sixteen 6mm bead caps
- One tube of 2mm bronze seed beads
- 3mm round metal beads

The bracelet
- Seven rounds of brown memory wire
- Three 4mm rings
- One metal tassel
- Two charms
- One tube of 2mm bronze seed beads
- Sixteen round 4mm metal beads

The earrings
- Two 6mm round dark red faceted beads
- Four 6mm bead caps
- Two big hoops
- Two hook ear wires
- Two 4mm rings
- Two filigree charms
- Four 4mm round metal beads
- Twenty-four 4mm bronze seed beads

Making the central plaque of the necklace

1 Use a laser printer or toner photocopier to print the "Fatma Hand" pattern. Draw over some details with the glitter gel pens. Cut around the pattern so you'll be able to center it on the clay more easily. A

2 Work one-quarter of the block of gold clay between your hands to soften it then form it into a sheet $1/8$ inch thick. Cut out a rectangle $1^1/2$ by 2 inches with a knife. Apply the printed pattern face down on the clay and press it with a clay roller; any air bubbles trapped between the paper and the clay will create a blank space in the design.

3 Texture the corners with the point of a needle and bake according to the manufacturer's instructions. B

4 For the best transfer, wait until the clay has cooled before gently peeling off the paper.

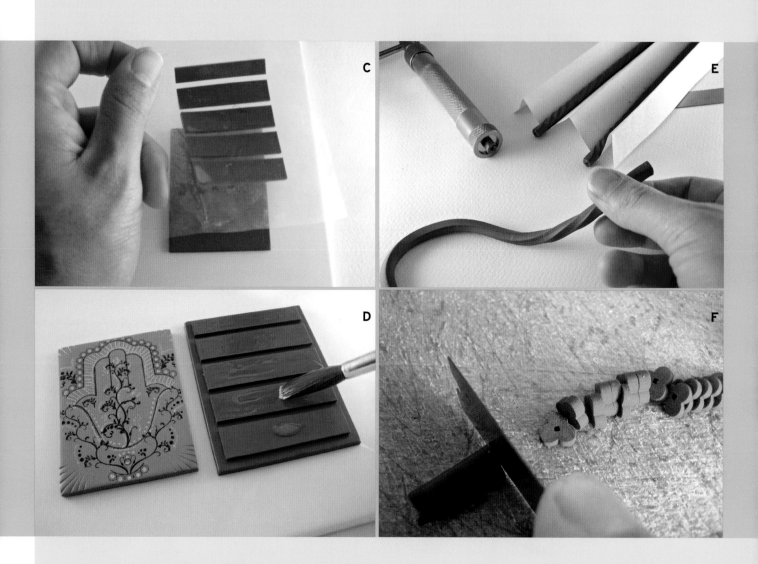

5 Work half a block of copper clay and make a very thin sheet then place it on a piece of cellophane. Cut out a rectangle 1¹/₂ by 2 inches. Use a knife to mark channels for the four wires then cut them out.

6 Place the parallel strips of clay on a copper sheet of the same thickness but a little bit larger (about ¹/₈ inch more all around). Press the parts together without marring the clay then gently pull away the cellophane. C

7 Apply a bit of liquid polymer clay on the copper bands and put the baked plaque with the pattern on top. D

ADVICE

At this stage, move your composition as little as possible. The liquid polymer clay doesn't act as glue until after baking, and the two parts risk sliding around if they are jostled.

8 Mix a bit of sparkly metallic powder into liquid polymer and apply this all around the hand. Bake according to the manufacturer's recommendations. Apply a second coat and bake again if you wish.

9 Once the piece has cooled completely, apply a coat of resin or varnish.

Making the beads

1 All the small beads are made the same way. Make a long tube, bake, and cut the beads just after they come out of the oven, when the clay is still warm and supple. To quickly make a long tube, use the clay gun with the appropriate attachment.

2 To make the long twisted beads, use a pentagon-shaped tip on the clay gun and create a long copper tube. Twist it and place it in paper folded like an accordion. Cut two lengths 8 inches each. E

G

3 With a paintbrush, apply a bit of copper powder then bake according to the manufacturer's instructions. After the clay comes out of the oven, cut it into sections, some 1/2 inch long, others slightly smaller.

4 The little burgundy spacers are made using a three-leaf-clover tip on the clay gun; cut thin slices from an 8-inch tube after baking. F

5 The little golden beads are made with a circular tip. The tube (two lengths of 8 inches) is twisted before baking. After it comes out of the oven, cut beads about 1/4 inch long.

6 The turquoise beads are made with a square tip. Cut some of them 1/4 inch long and others, twisted before baking, 1/2 inch long. To give this color a more natural look, make a light marble with the turquoise and some brown before placing in the clay gun. Make two lengths of 8 inches.

7 From the burgundy clay, make four oval beads. For these, start with a sphere and then mold it into an olive shape in the palms of your hands.

Assembling the necklace
Refer to the pattern for assembly (G).

Assembling the bracelet
Make a loop on one of the ends of the wire and attach the tassel with a ring. Thread on the polymer beads and the seed beads. Be careful to spread out the sizes and colors of the beads. Finish the bracelet by making a loop on the wire and attach two charms with a ring.

Assembling the earrings
On a large hoop, string on the beads in a symmetrical fashion and close the hoop by twisting the wire with pliers. Attach the charm using a ring and add the hook ear wires.

A baroque look

Metal stamps applied directly into the clay give this necklace the look of an ancient piece of jewelry.

Materials for the beads

- One block of violet clay
- Quarter block of vermillion clay
- Copper metallic powder
- Liquid Fimo clay
- Red alcohol ink
- Textured sheet
- Fine salt
- Varnish
- Rectangular metal filigree piece, 1½ by 1 inch long
- Two large filigree links
- Eye-shaped cookie cutter, 1 inch long
- Cling wrap

Materials for assembly

- Beading wire, 3 or 4 feet
- Four flat filigree and imitation crystal beads with loops on the back to let the wire pass through
- Twelve 4mm copper bead caps
- Two 12mm copper bead caps
- 2mm bronze seed beads
- 2mm red seed beads
- 3mm frosted amethyst seed beads
- Thirty-two 4mm alexandrite crystal bicones
- Eight 4mm bronze faceted beads
- Two bead tips
- Two rings
- One clasp
- One extension chain
- Jewelry glue

Making the beads

1 In a sheet of violet clay ⅛ inch thick, covered with cling wrap (to produce rounded edges), cut out two eye shapes with the cookie cutter (A). Push the filigree link into the clay, on the baking surface. B

2 For the pendant, make a slightly thicker sheet of violet clay, lay it on the baking surface, and print the surface with the textured sheet.

3 Press the filigree rectangle into the clay, taking care not to crush the raised pattern.

4 With a flexible blade, trim around the metal sheet in gentle curves, leaving ¼ inch of textured clay all the way around.

5 With a bit of vermillion clay, make four tiny beads and attach them around the center of the medallion, gluing them in place with a drop of liquid polymer clay. Pierce the bead before baking without deforming it and leave the metal pin inside until after the piece is baked.

6 Make four vermillion salt beads (see page 17 for instructions) and two round beads covered with bronze powder.

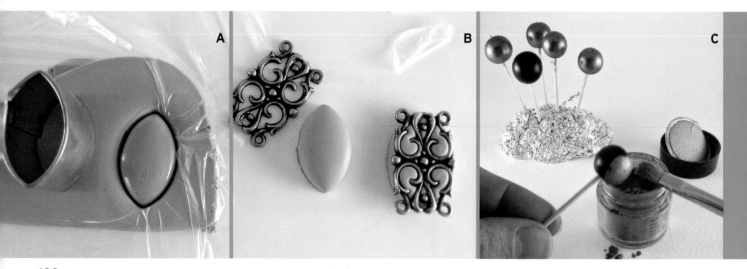

A   B   C

7 Put some bronze powder on the edge of the pendant and the textured border. D

8 Mix a bit of liquid polymer with a drop of red ink and fill in the center of the metal piece with the mixture. E

Finishing the beads

Sand the backs of the beads. Apply varnish on the parts covered with metallic powder as well as on the center of the pendant.

Assembling the necklace

1 Begin by placing a small seed bead in the middle of the wire. Fold the wire in two around the bead and put the ends through the bead tip so that the seed bead ends up inside it. Follow the pattern for stringing the beads. F

2 When you get to the end, block off the ends of the wires by pinching them in a crimp bead after the last faceted bead, then trap a second crimp bead inside a bead tip. Cut the ends of the wires off close and add a drop of glue before closing the bead tip.

A festive look

A succession of crystal cabochons and gold-foil beads make this an excellent necklace for a party.

Materials for the beads

- Two blocks of sparkly red clay
- One block of gold clay
- One block of black
- Six sheets of gold foil
- Alcohol ink in several shades of red
- One round cookie cutter, ¾ inch diameter
- One oval cookie cutter, 1 by ¾ inch
- Cellophane
- Coarse sandpaper
- Gedeo crystal resin
- Two dark red 10mm crystal cabochons
- Two dark red 12mm crystal cabochons
- Two dark red 18mm crystal cabochons
- One decorated bronze setting for the oval cabochon
- Heat-resistant glue
- Two-part epoxy
- Eleven ½-inch glue-on metal bead backs with channels for the wire
- Matte black model paint

Materials for assembly

- Hollow burgundy velvet cord, 12 inches
- Several bronze seed beads
- Two 4mm dark red faceted matte-finish glass beads
- One gold clasp and two rings
- 20-gauge brass wire, 12 inches

Making the beads

The striped sheet

1 Make two squares of gold clay and four squares of sparkly red clay, all ⅛ inch thick, and put a sheet of gold foil on each one. A

2 Apply red ink to the gold foil on one of the gold squares and on three of the red squares. Try to create different nuances of color by playing with several kinds of ink or putting on multiple coats to get a darker color. Let the ink dry completely before continuing. B

3 Put your squares through the clay machine on the ⅛-inch setting–this will produce horizontal cracks. Then do it again, making the opening one notch smaller, first turning the sheets a quarter turn.

4 Cut each sheet into strips about ⅛ inch thick. Try to make the strips identical. C

5 Roll out a sheet ⅛ inch thick with the red clay and place the strips on top, alternating the colors.

6 Use your knife to position the strips. This will allow you to push each strip right up next to its neighbor.

7 Once you have all the strips placed, lay a piece of cellophane on the surface (this will prevent the gold foil from coming off) and gently smooth the clay with a roller, first in one direction, then the other.

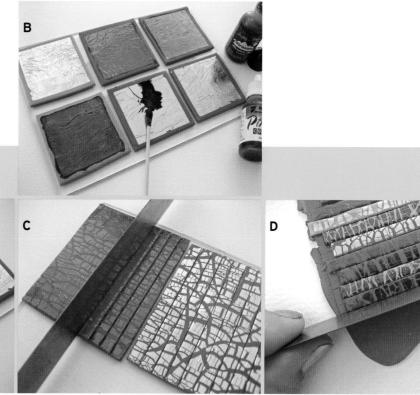

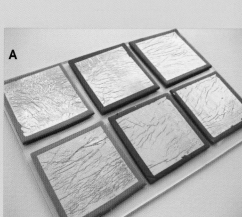

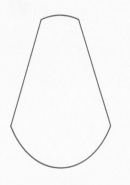

Assembling the pendants

1 Place one sheet of black clay ¹/₈ thick on the baking surface, taking care to not create any air pockets. Texture the surface by pressing it with a piece of coarse-grain sandpaper.

2 Cut out eleven ovals with a cookie cutter (or use the pattern given here) and take away the extra scraps. Next, put the pattern on the oval and cut off the excess parts. Create eleven identical shapes in this way. E

3 On four of these shapes, place a circle of sparkly red clay ³/₄ inch in diameter;

on one other, an oval. Hollow out the centers before placing the crystal cabochons. F

4 Put a bit of heat-resistant glue under the cabochons before putting them in place: the two small ones and the two medium-sized ones on the circles, and the oval in its metal setting on the bead of the same shape.

5 Texture the edge with dashes made with the point of a needle then hollow out little circles between each of them. G

6 Emphasize the relief by putting gold powder on the border using the tip of your finger. Be careful not to go onto the black clay.

7 Cut six circles out of the striped sheet with a cookie cutter and put them on the remaining black shapes. Press down without deforming the clay.

8 Bake according to the manufacturer's instructions.

Finishing the beads

1 Sand the backs and edges of the beads.

2 Apply varnish on the parts dusted in gold powder and resin on the parts with gold foil.

3 Once the beads are very dry, attach the metal bead backs to the back of each bead using two-part epoxy. When the backs are firmly glued, paint them with black model paint.

Assembling the necklace

1 From the velvet tubing, cut sections ¹/₄ inch long and place them between all the pendants (H). For a prettier look, you can put a seed bead at both ends of each of these tubes.

2 Finish the remainder of the necklace with a 2 ³/₄-inch velvet tube on each side. Add a faceted bead at each end then make a loop in the wire and attach the ring for the clasp. I

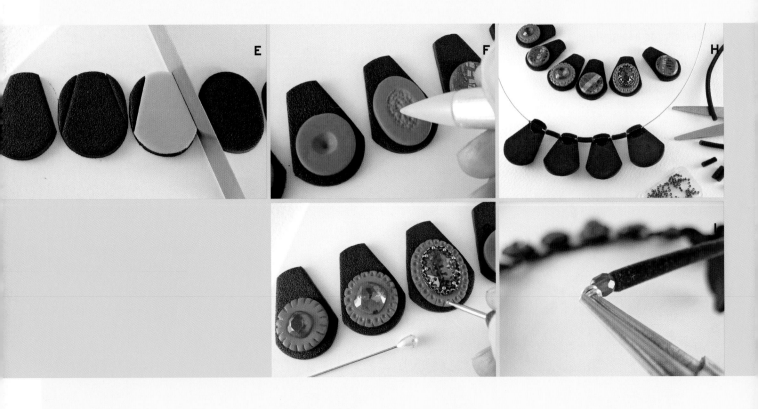

A flowery look

This necklace combines a crackle finish and flower cane designs—the ring, made with resin, highlights depth.

Materials for the beads

- One block of copper clay
- One flower cane in three sizes (see page 28)
- Gold foil
- Cellophane
- Cling wrap
- Round cookie cutters, ¾, 1, and 1¼ inches in diameter

Materials for assembly

The necklace (see page 131)

- Nine decorated rings, with holes on each side that a 6mm bead can fit inside
- Ten headpins
- One clasp and two rings
- Beading wire, two 16-inch strands
- Nine 6mm bronze-colored pearly beads
- Eight large (8mm) faceted crystal beads with gold centers
- Twenty 4mm bronze-colored faceted beads
- Bronze seed beads
- Four crimp beads
- Drill, ³⁄₆₄-inch bit

The necklace beads

1 On a sheet of copper clay ⅛ inch thick, apply a sheet of cane about 1 inch in diameter and smooth it out with a roller. Cut it out with a circular cookie cutter directly on the baking surface. Make two identical beads. A

2 On a sheet ⅛ inch thick, apply slices of the flower cane. Cover a surface large enough that you can cut out two 1-inch circles. Make the thin slices overlap and balance the opaque parts and the transparent parts. Smooth it out with a roller then cut out 1-inch circles with a cookie cutter. A

3 On a sheet of copper clay ⅛ inch thick, apply a sheet of gold foil, taking care to smooth out any air bubbles with the tip of your finger. B

4 Set the clay machine one notch thinner and run the sheet through again. Turn it a quarter turn and put it through the machine again, on an even thinner setting.

5 Cut two circles out with the smallest circular cookie cutter and place each on a larger copper circle. Also cut out two circles 1 inch in diameter and place them on a sheet ⅛ inch thick. Make the two layers stick together by pressing down with a sheet of glass or Plexiglas then cut the circles out again directly on the baking surface if they were deformed during the pressing.

6 From a medium-sized (about 1 inch in diameter) flower cane, cut two very thin slices and trim away the translucent triangles between the petals. D

Attach a flower to the side of each crackled-gold-foil disk, one on the right side and the other on the left. Press lightly with a sheet of glass to make them stick without deforming them.

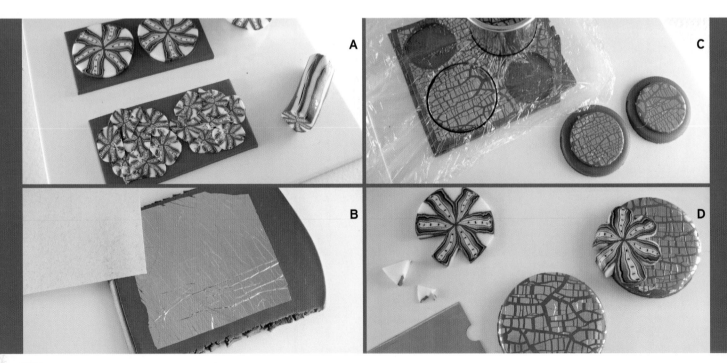

7 From the 1-inch flower cane, cut a very thin slice and trim off the translucent angles.

8 Put this flower on the center of a small ball of clay with a needle poked through it. Give it a pretty shape, molding its petals. E

9 The center bead is unique, and a bit larger than the others. On a sheet $\frac{1}{8}$ inch thick, make a background with the smaller flower canes slices and add a slice of the larger flower cane. Smooth it out and cut out a circle $1\frac{1}{2}$ inches in diameter, placing the large flower a bit to the side.

Finishing the beads

1 Bake according to the manufacturer's instructions. Sand the backs of the beads and the parts not covered in gold foil. Apply varnish on the gold-foil parts. Keep a matte finish, with the flowers in relief.

2 Make holes in the beads about $\frac{1}{8}$ inch from the edges in the upper quarter of the beads. F

 ADVICE

To be certain to position the holes in an even fashion, use a circle of paper as a template. Then all you will need to do is press with the point of a needle, then lift up the paper to pierce them in the right spot.

Assembling the necklace

1 Put a headpin through the right hole of the flat clay flower bead. Add a ring of twisted metal with a pearly bead on the inside and finish with a loop. G

2 Put a headpin through the hole on the left side of the bead, coming out at the front of the bead, then add the metal ring with the pearly bead and the next polymer clay bead (the crackled round bead with the flower). H

3 Cut the pin $\frac{1}{4}$ inch away from the hole then twist it at a 90-degree angle to the back of the bead. Finish by making a loop and pressing it down against the clay surface. I

4 Continue in the same way with all the beads of the necklace, putting in the molded flower instead of the seventh ring and pearly bead (counting from the left).

5 Once all the beads are attached, add a beading wire folded in two on each side and string on the large faceted beads, then the small ones, separated by seed beads.

6 Finish with two crimp beads, forming a loop to attach the ring. J

The ring

Materials

- One ring base with a flat surface
- Two-part crystal resin
- Gloves
- Disposable plastic container
- Wooden stick
- Half-sphere silicone mold, 1 inch in diameter

1 Make two flowers in different sizes (one 1 inch and one ½ inch) with slices of cane. Cut out the transparent clay from between the petals and round them. Bake according to the manufacturer's instructions.

2 To cast the ring, you'll need a silicone mold with a shiny inside. Generally, these molds are used for cooking; you can easily find them on the internet or in craft-supply stores.

3 Prepare the resin following the instructions. Pour half of it into the mold.
4 Soak the smaller flower in the resin, let the excess drip off, then place it in the bottom of the mold, taking care to not create air bubbles.

Proceed in the same fashion for the large flower, which will settle slightly above the first.

Wait about two hours for the resin to begin to set.
5 Prepare the ring base and open the hooks. Place it on the large flower and

ADVICE

To avoid creating bubbles, it's better to soak the elements in the resin before putting them in place.

add a little bit of resin, if necessary, so that the flat part of the ring is completely covered. Wait twenty-four hours before taking it out of the mold.
6 Sand the edges lightly, wearing a face mask for protection from the dust.

some notes on color

Lighting

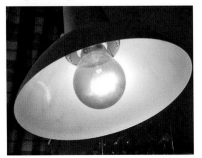

To see colors clearly, your workspace must have good and sufficient lighting. The look of colors can vary widely depending on how they are lit. It is wise to buy a "daylight" bulb for your work area; such bulbs can usually be used with any lamp. They create a brightness very close to natural light, which will allow you to see the true colors of your work. These bulbs can be found at most home centers. More expensive natural lighting systems can also be found at craft stores.

The color wheel

Some crafters are naturally adept at creating beautiful color combinations. For many others, this skill is harder to come by. The color wheel is a great tool to help you come up with appealing color combinations and avoid less-

appealing schemes. Wheels are available at craft centers and art stores.

There are three primary colors: blue, red, and yellow. They are called primary because they cannot be created by mixing and are a part of other colors. In theory, you can obtain every other color from them. In reality, though, pigments can sometimes create a chemical reaction that alters color, making them appear duller than you think they should. This effect can be minor—but it's still wise to fill out your collection of clay with colors other than just blue, red, and yellow.

When you mix two primary colors, you get what's called a secondary color.

- yellow + blue = green
- yellow + red = orange
- red + blue = purple

Primary and secondary colors are vivid colors, called "saturated." When you mix a primary color with the secondary color that's next to it on the wheel, you get an intermediate color. For example: yellow + green = green-yellow.

If you add black, white, or gray to a color—or a little of its complement (see below)—you will create what's called a "desaturated" color.

Complementary colors

Complementary colors are those that are directly opposite each other on the color wheel.

- The complement of yellow is purple
- The complement of red is green
- The complement of blue is orange

It's important to know the complements of colors; they can be used to create many different effects: softening your colors without dulling them, creating a harmony or contrast, evening out a composition . . . bringing to it a spark.

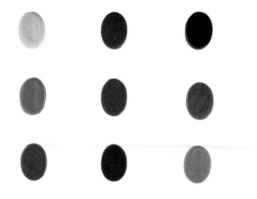

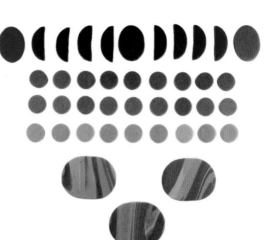

When you mix a color with its complement, you get a tint less luminous that actually tends toward brown, especially as you add more of the complement. Adding complementary colors sparingly is important so the color doesn't get too brown and become scrap.

If you proceed very methodically, however, you can create a range of wonderful nuances. And if you add white, the color will become clearer; varying amounts of white will create very subtle differences.

Contrasts

The contrast of values puts a light color and a dark color in opposition. The most striking case is the contrast between black and white.

When you place two complementary colors side by side, you will get a vibrant effect with good contrast—a desirable effect that makes the colors striking without one or the other being overwhelming.

Harmony

When you progressively add white or black to a color, you will get what's called a monochrome—various shades of just

one color. This collection of nuances can be used to create jewelry with appealing harmony: discretely colored pieces that have depth and a subtle beauty.

As well, the colors next to each other on the color wheel will create an equally harmonious color scheme.

Appealing associations

Brown can work well with a number of colors:

- pink (see page 92)
- green (see page 94)
- blue (see page 98)

This is also the case with black, white, and gray.

Patterns

For the project on page 116

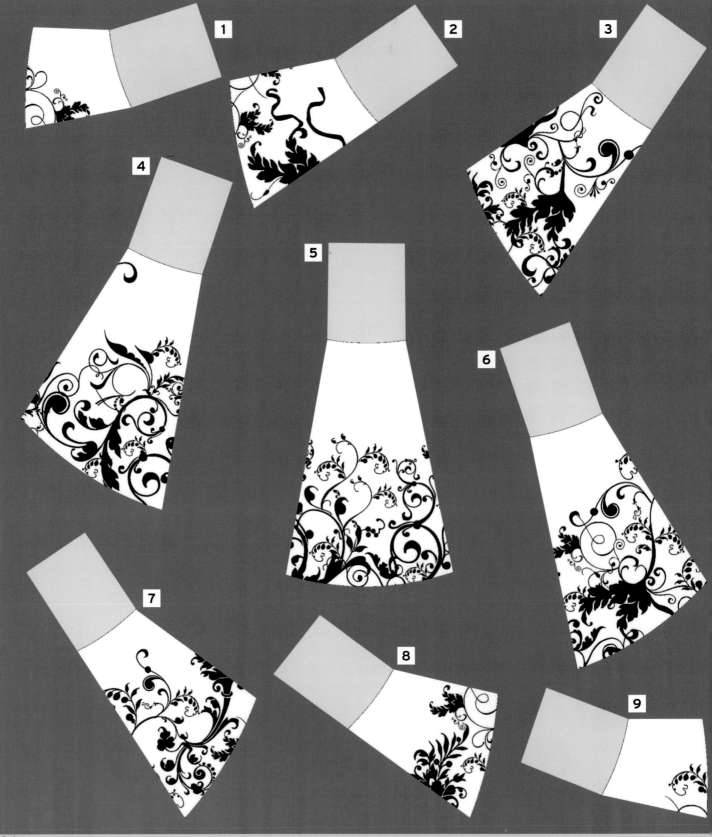

Glossary

Bead roller: plastic mold tool used by clay crafters to make a quantity of beads all the exact same size.

Buna cord: rubber cord, solid or hollow.

Cane: see *millefiori*.

Clay gun: syringelike tool that uses different tips that makes ropes of clay with a particular form and creates effects with color in canes; this is much easier to use than a screw thread.

Clay shaper: paintbrushlike tool with a rubber tip instead of bristles used to shape or smooth clay.

Condition: preparing the clay before work to give it a homogeneous temperature and consistency.

Heat gun: electric embosser, a heat tool used to quickly bake a layer of liquid polymer or small polymer pieces or to perform little repairs; must be used with care.

Hidden Magic: variation of mokume gane.

Inclusions: elements introduced into raw clay (embossing powders, sand, gold foil, microbeads, and so on).

Mica shift: technique that creates ghostlike effects in pearly clay (see page 23).

Millefiori or **millefiori cane:** roll of clay containing an identical pattern from one end to the other; the cane is cut into slices for use on jewelry.

Mokume gane: effect created by layering different colored sheets of clay, imprinting them, then shaving off portions to reveal the underlying pattern; inspired by an ancient Japanese metalworking technique.

Pearl-ex: common name for a fine, volatile powder that creates colored effects—pearly or metallic—in polymer clay; many different brands (Jacquard, Fimo, Ranger, and others) are available. Paper-crafters' embossing powder, used to create raised patterns when heated, is equally compatible with polymer clay.

Push mold: rigid mold into which clay is pressed to give it a particular form; different brands are available.

Reducing a cane: technique for elongating a cylinder of patterned clay; proper reducing makes the diameter smaller while retaining the pattern throughout the entire length of clay.

Scrap: excess clay that can be used to make the core of round beads or unique molds.

Skinner Blend: technique invented by Judith Skinner to created shaded sheets of clay with the help of a clay machine.

Texturize: giving a raised pattern to raw clay through the use of different tools.

Transfer: reproduction of a printed image directly onto clay. This can be done by simple contact with the raw clay or by using polymer liquid or transfer paper meant for T-shirts.

Watercolor mosaic: a colorful effect for beads created by layering a colored sheet of clay, a white sheet, and a black sheet, tearing the clay into little pieces, then reforming it into beads.